# This is our story…
Edgar and Katie King

A Life of Hard Work, Love and Salvation

By Edgar King

© Copyright 2022 Edgar King – All rights reserved.

It is not legal to reproduce, duplicate, or transmit any part of this document in either electronic means or printed format. Recording of this publication is strictly prohibited.

Published by PlashMill Press, Scotland.

ISBN: 978-1-9993620-3-4

This book is dedicated to my children, Mike, Yvette, Michelle and Rochelle and my seven grandchildren, Connor Odea, Miranda Dell'Anna, Rachel Dell 'Anna, Sammy Bowers. Ashleigh Smith, Chantelle Smith, Joshua Smith.

I wrote this story so that my grandchildren would have an insight into my life story and the King family.

Figure 1. My younger brother Harry, with Elsie Lefrense. Harry had Down syndrome, which wasn't acknowledged back in the fifties. Harry passed away at the age of ten, a year after my dad died.

Table of Contents

A SOLDIER IN TWO ARMIES. 1

Chapter 1 – From Bay D'Espoir to a Broken Family   3

Chapter 2 – Working Hard and Playing Hard   23

Chapter 3 - My Electrifying Career (and Music and Love)   31

Chapter 4 – My Years in Uniform   39

Chapter 5 – Finding Salvation with My Family   59

Chapter 6 - Blazing New Trails   69

Chapter 7 - Our First Salvation Army Appointments   85

Chapter 8 – Entering the Field of Corrections   99

Chapter 9 – Chaplains in Kingston, even to Clifford Olson   113

Chapter 10 – A Fresh Start in Our Work and Family   129

Chapter 11 – The Peterborough Years   145

Chapter 12 – Navigating Rough Seas in Halifax   163

Chapter 13 – Fighting Cancer   173

Chapter 14 – New Assignments and Relationships   191

A SOLDIER IN TWO ARMIES.

I served in the Canadian Military with the Royal Canadian Engineers in the sixties. I trained with the Queens Own Rifles in Calgary, Alberta.

After my marriage to my wife, Katie Harris, I received an Honourable release from the military, and moved back to Newfoundland.

A year later my wife Katie and I started a spiritual journey together. We made a commitment to ministry in The Salvation Army. Katie and I were ordained/commissioned as Salvation Army officers, with the rank of lieutenants.

We served in Newfoundland for five years, in two corps appointments. Two years in Mings Bight and Three years in Greens Harbour , serving as corps officers/pastors.

We were transferred to The Salvation Army Correctional Services in Edmonton, Alberta, in 1981. Afterward, we served in other provinces across Canada with the Salvation Army Correctional service department.

Katie passed away in Pentiction, British Columbia, in 1999 while we were the pastors at the corps.

After twenty-seven years of active service, I retired in 2003, with the rank of major.

After retirement I worked for the Salvation Army as a chaplain in the super jail in Lindsay, Ontario. Later, I went to work at the super jail in Penetanguishene, Ontario, also as a chaplain.

I also worked as an electronic specialist for The Salvation Army, installing ankle bracelets on clients for the home arrest program. Clients were monitored at home instead of being incarcerated in an institution.

My journey has been interesting to say the least.

Chapter 1 – From Bay D'Espoir to a Broken Family

I was born in Isle-aux-Morts, Newfoundland, on August 26, 1945, to Ted (Edwin) and Dorothy King. My parents and four siblings had moved from Morrisville, Bay D'Espoir around 1944 when my father was employed by Fishery Products International to work as an engineer on the fish plant in Isle-aux-Morts. We were classed as British subjects back then as Newfoundland didn't join Canada until 1949.

My father had one brother, Abraham King, and two sisters, Elizabeth and Elsie. My father was born in McCallum, an isolated community on the southwest coast. People still reside there today but it is not connected by road, only by boat.

My mother was Dorothy Taylor. Her mother was Charity Jane Kendell. The Kendells were the first settlers in Morrisville. They owned and operated a large sawmill and were the main employer and merchant in the community. Back then people worked at the sawmill, and purchased food, clothing, and whatever they needed at the Kendell store. There was no money exchanged back then, the merchants were the only people who had any form of currency.

My father was not happy with the employment situation in Morrisville, so he decided to go to Grand Falls and look for employment with Bowater's. After being employed there for a number of weeks he returned to Morrisville and showed the men at the sawmill what it meant to work for real money. A number of men from the mill went with him to Grand Falls and were employed with Bowaters. This did not go over well with the Kendell family. My grandmother Charity Kendell was married to Thomas Taylor, they had four sons, Lionel, Cyril, Jack and Ralph, and also two daughters, Dorothy and

Harriett. Three of the Taylor boys served in the military during the Second World War.

Morrisville is still a small community with mostly retired senior citizens. They must go outside the community for groceries and other service requirements.

This is the only photo I have of both my parents Dorothy (second from left) and Ted (right) in the same image. They are with her brother and mother.

Isle-aux-Morts was a little fishing community on the Southwest Coast of Newfoundland. It was located around sixteen kilometres from

Port-Aux-Basque. The first settlers in Isle-aux-Morts were the Harvey family, George and Ann Harvey. In 1828, the Harvey family rescued 163 people from the French ship, the *Dispatch*, shipwrecked on the rocks off Isle-aux-Morts. Those who perished were buried on the island, and the French referred to it as the Island of Death, Isle-aux-Morts. The Harveys moved to the main part of the island and continued to call it Isle-aux-Morts.

The only way to this community was by boat, as it was not connected by road.

Fishery Products International was the main employer in the community. Men and women worked on the fish plant processing the fish that was supplied by schooners and skiffs in the early forties.

After Newfoundland joined Canada, the fish plant expanded, and larger boats, trawlers and long liners, supplied the plant with fish. It was one of the largest fish plants on the Southwest Coast. There were two main sections in the plant, the cutting room where the fish were filleted by men, and the packing area that employed mostly women, who packed the fish in different size boxes before it was moved to the cold storage after freezing. After a large quantity of fish was processed and frozen, Fishery Products International had a large cargo ship that took the fish and delivered it to different markets around the world.

The company provided a house for our family located down in the barachois, a shallow tidal lagoon. I was born in the house, delivered by a midwife, Aunt Polly Scott. I had three older brothers and a sister, Frank, Ken, Cas, and Winnie. My younger brother Harry was also born at home, delivered by the same midwife around 1947. He had Down Syndrome, but no one knew what that was at the time. He was slow advancing as a child, could not talk clearly and had a lot of health issues, so he did not attend school. We were very close, and had fun playing together, even though he was limited in some ways. That house, so full of good memories, no longer exists. It was torn down and a marine slipway was built on the land.

The low building in the middle of the photo on the left was my childhood home. It has since been torn down, as I discovered when I visited and found this empty space.

I learned to swim in the barachois in the summer and skate on it in the winter. It was deep when the tide was high. Salt water was great to swim in since you float better than in fresh water. We didn't have playgrounds or recreation facilities like children have today. We played outside and entertained each other with games that we all could enjoy. We played hopscotch, ball, and other games together. I remember having a wire hoop that I pushed around with a straight piece of wire, almost all boys had one. We also cut boughs for Bonfire Night; we would gather them for months so we could have a large bonfire. The only way around the community was on a footpath. It was just a narrow walking trail, there were no bikes back then, until the road was built. I remember there was a pond by the fish plant, that was dammed off to supply fresh water to the plant. The upper end of the pond was a wet bog that you couldn't walk on because you would sink in the mud.

As a small boy around five or six, I was by the pond picking what we called bread and butter plants, you plucked them from the ground and could eat the root of the plant. There were large plants by the pond. I went close to the upper end where it was muddy, turned my back to the water and pulled up a plant. I lost my balance and fell into the muddy pond. There were no adults around to help me. I managed to roll over in the mud on my stomach and slowly crawled back on the bank. I never went there again after getting a scare and realized how serious it could have been. Years later a young child drowned there.

My mother played the organ in the Anglican church and we had a pump organ in our home. Canon Martin, the Anglican minister, would visit from Port-Aux-Basque and would go over the hymns that he wanted to use when he did a service.

My father was not only an engineer on the fish plant, but also an entrepreneur. He had a small home-based business, making and selling concrete chimneys. He also sold Bibles in different sizes and colours that people could order. He enjoyed doing this in his spare time. As a boy, I remember going with him in a row dory to a cove for sand that he used for making chimneys. He made moulds for the cement blocks with different size for the stove pipes. I always enjoyed watching him mixing the cement and putting it in moulds to make the different size chimneys. When the cement was hardened, he would remove the chimney blocks from the moulds and set them up for another refill. He always kept busy on his days off and loved his hobby.

He enjoyed his work at the fish plant as an engineer. In those days, if an engine broke down, they had to improvise, as it could be difficult getting parts to repair them. Today it is so different, not much is repaired, usually parts are replaced with new ones. There were several engineers working different shifts as the fish plant was a twenty-four-hour operation. I remember Maty Ball, Jack Lafosse and Mark Janes worked there also. Engineering was a skill that was of interest to my brothers also. My older brother Frank in later years was an engineer on the fish plant and became the chief engineer. My brother Cas was in the military with the Royal Canadian Engineers. I also served in the military with the Royal Canadian Engineers.

We were very creative as a family; my

brother Ken was an agent for tailor made clothes. When someone decided to get married, they wanted a suit. My brother Ken would take their measurements, send them in to the company and they would receive their suit in the mail. He received a commission for each suit he sold. Ken was also very creative in exploring how things worked, like flashlights and other items, and always tried to make them more powerful and better.

While working at the fish plant as an engineer, my father (shown at right) had an accident that injured his stomach. They had a diesel motor up on a chain hoist and he was under it, taking the bolts out of the

base pan. The chain hoist slipped and pinned him to the floor. There was no |doctor in the community, so he continued to rest at home, but over time he became very ill.

He was admitted to the hospital in Port-Aux-Basque. The only way we could visit was by boat, since there wasn't a road between the two towns back then. His stomach was sore for months. He became very ill and did not recover.

I remember Jim Baggs, the owner of a skiff, taking my mother, Elizer Seymour and me to Port-Aux-Basque to visit my father in the hospital. The sea was rough so they put me down in the forecastle so I would not be washed off the deck by the rough sea. Several fishermen would transport my mother and me to Port-Aux-Basque while my father was very ill before he passed away. Lory Seymour took us once on his long liner, the *Zany*.

My father was diagnosed with cancer and passed away around 1955 at the young age of forty-nine. My oldest brother Frank was in the military, and Cas also enlisted in the army. Ken stayed home and got married shortly after my father's death.

My brother Frank got an honourable release from the military and came home to train as an engineer on the fish plant to help support our family because we were going through a difficult time after our father passed away.

We were like a ship drifting at sea without a captain. Our family was broken, and the future didn't look good.

A year after my father passed away, my younger brother Harry died in the late hours of the night. I remember my mother coming into the room and taking him off the bed. I didn't realize that he had died in bed next to me.

We were devastated by going through another loss in the family. All the happiness we shared felt like it was gone. We were lost, with no light at the end of the tunnel.

We were in a difficult situation, living in survival mode. My mother received a widow's allowance of $30 a month from the government. It was impossible to survive on this small income and keep the household going. There was never enough to go around. We had to settle for second best in most things. Because we were on a widows' allowance, we were treated like people on welfare. I remember how we couldn't afford new school books, so we were given used books that other students discarded.

It was humiliating to say the least, to be treated like second class citizens because of our circumstances. It changed our whole way of life, that affected us through the years ahead.

A family in Isle-aux-Morts offered to adopt me, as they had no children, but my mother said no. Her children were her responsibility.

A man in Corner Brook, Jim Legge, was looking for a housekeeper, so my mother looked into it and decided to accept the offer. She moved to Corner Brook with me and my sister Winnie. We didn't know anything about this man, except that he worked at the Bowater's Mill.

We went by train from Port-Aux-Basque to Corner Brook and started a new journey as a broken family. Legge told us we were going to live on the lower end of Pier Road, but after arriving we found out his house was in Crow Gulch. Due to the stigma of that area, he had lied about the location. As I look back over the years, I realize the people of Crow Gulch were treated unfairly and with cruelty by people of Corner Brook. I had many friends there, including close friends Alphonse Bennett, John Ryan, and Malcolm and Arthur Campbell.

I went to the public school on Broadway and registered as living on Pier Road. This helped me avoid the stigma regarding people who lived in Crow Gulch. My teacher was Miss

Janes, who was in her senior years. One day she asked me to take her shoes to the cobbler on Country Road for repairs. I didn't know at the time who the cobbler was; years later I found out he was Major Bill Reader's father (Major Reader was a Salvation Army officer whom I came to know years later.)

We lived there for a year and a half, then Legge sold his house in Crow Gulch to the Campbell family. We then moved back to his hometown of St. David's, where his father and brother lived. He quit his job at the mill and started fishing in St. George's Bay.

It was a different lifestyle than living in Crow Gulch, as we were now in the farming area. We lived on an acreage and had a horse for hauling wood. It was my responsibility to look after it, making sure it was fed and watered, while also cleaning the barn. Our horse's name was Colonel, he was a large white horse that weighed around 1800 lbs.

St David's was a small community and

not as busy as it was in Corner Brook. We lived in an old two-story house. The lower level was completed, but the upstairs was open, no partitions, or insulation. My bed was upstairs and very cold in the winter. The house was heated by a wood stove downstairs that did not heat the upstairs section. As I look back over the years I am amazed that I survived this depressing lifestyle.

I remember one day I decided to ride our horse bare back to a spring so it could drink the clear spring water. Before I got to the spring, my friend Donald Chaffey was roping a fence post with a piece of six thread rope. He said to me,

"Bet you can't rope the post on horseback!"

I took the challenge, wrapped the rope around my left hand and started to ride the horse. First try I roped the post but when I tried to stop the horse, he spooked and took off. I was pulled off the horse with the rope that was caught around my hand. I landed on the ground and realized the rope had caught two of my fingers. It had severely burned the top off my little finger and severed my other finger. I ran home scared and my mother got Lewin Gilliam to drive us to the clinic in Jeffrey's.

My fingers were injured so severely that the doctor sent us to the hospital in Stephenville, as he couldn't do anything to repair the wounds. They stitched the top back on my little finger and stitched the other finger. It was months before I could go back to school. That was the last time I rode our horse bareback.

I missed my home in Isle-aux-Morts where my brother Ken was living in our house. In the summer I would visit and it felt like I was back home again down in the barachois. During the summer I would get a job at the fish plant, picking worms out of cod fillets or working on the skinning machine and other tasks. I think we got around sixty-five cents an hour. It was always exciting for me to go back to Isle-aux-Morts and live in the house that I was born in.

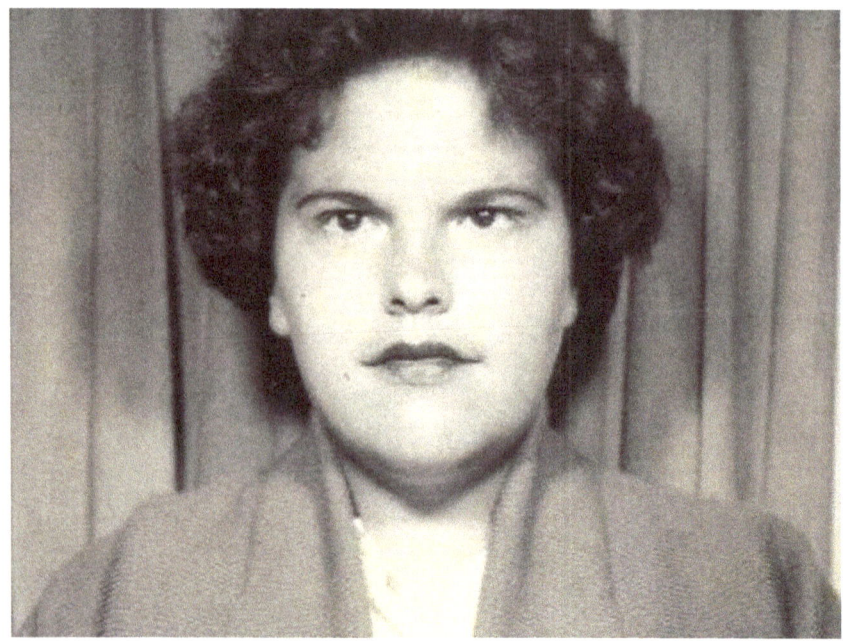

My sister Winnie May Harvey was married to Jim Harvey of Isle-aux-Morts, Jim is a descendant of George and Ann Harvey, the first settlers in Isle-aux-Morts.

While I was back in Isle-aux-Morts one summer, I got word that my mother was having a hard time in St. David's with Jim Legge. He didn't treat us very well. He was verbally and physically abusive and controlled us like a piece of property. We felt trapped with nowhere to go. We were trying to survive daily. I think my mother waited until I was back in Isle-aux-Morts before she decided to leave this abusive situation.

Around 1960, while I was in Isle-aux-Morts, things started to fall apart and Mom finally decided to leave. She was devastated, with nowhere to go; she didn't want to be a burden to her family. Nora French took her in and encouraged her to contact Silas Hulan. He had a large family and needed someone to look after them. His wife had passed away after giving birth to their eleventh child.

She moved in with the Hulan family and took the responsibility of caring for the five children who were still at home. The youngest were Debbie, Verna, Hillard, Junior, and Winston. She later married Silas and I acquired eleven stepsiblings.

She finally found a place where she was appreciated, Silas treated her with respect and was happy to have her there looking after his family. I was welcomed into the family and soon felt at home living there.

Silas gave me a piece of land on his property in St. David's, with title ownership to it. I later sold it to a family who bought the house we lived in after Silas passed away.

I still have contact with the Hulan family in Newfoundland.

Chapter 2 – Working Hard and Playing Hard

When I was fifteen, Mom and my stepfather Silas wanted me to come back to St. David's and go back to school to start Grade 9. I didn't want to continue with school but decided to move back with them and get a job in the woods, cutting pulp wood for Bowater with Junior. We had a bucksaw each and, after eighteen days, our wood was scaled. We went to Doyle's store and bought a Pioneer chain saw from Mike Martin.

I worked in the woods for a couple of years, cutting pulpwood. I didn't make a lot of money and the work was hard. I then went to work with Charlie Alley on his truck, hauling pulpwood from River Brook and loading it on railway cars at the landing in Jeffreys. We were getting paid around $12.05 a day for working nine hours a day.

Then things started to change. The owner of the truck wanted three loads per day before I was paid for the nine hours. At times, there were problems with the truck so he decided if we only made two  loads, I would only get paid for six hours, even though it took us nine hours to get the two loads to the siding. We were unionized so I questioned him regarding paying me by the load instead of for the hours we worked. He made an issue of it, so I contacted our union representative about my situation. He said he would investigate it and get back to me. The owner of the truck told me it was his choice, so I did not work for him anymore.

The union rep, in consulting with the contractor, decided to put me on the landing, helping other trucks load wood. This lasted for about a week, then I was laid off by the contractor with no reference to the issue about the truck. I was disappointed with the union since I felt like I had been thrown under the bus. I later went to work with Carl Chaffey, another private truck owner. He paid me for the full hours I worked. It was great working with Carl, and he always appreciated my work.

We always made hay every summer for our horse, in a field down by Crabbe's River. One day, after we finished, we drove back home with John Osmond in his car. When we got to the railroad crossing, a train came down the grade and blasted its horn. Our friend John Osmond, who was driving, panicked and hit the gas instead of the brake. We shot across the track in front of the train and up the side of the bank. It was quite a scare. Needless to say we weren't hungry when we got home, because of it.

We had an outdoor ice rink in St. David's, where I played a lot of hockey in the winter. We played other teams in the area and enjoyed it very much. A few guys wouldn't play as they worked in the woods for a living and didn't want to get hurt.

I was tired of working in the woods and decided that it was time to look elsewhere for employment. Premier Joey Smallwood started a new training program in St. John's called the Fisheries College. I applied and got accepted in the engineering program, referred to as Marine Engineering.

My older brother Frank was a stationary engineer at the plant in Isle-aux Morts so I was extremely interested in the program and that career. After finishing the first year, I had to wait as the program ended before starting up again in September.

During the first semester, all students stayed at Fort Pepperell, the old American barracks that were closed after the Americans left

Newfoundland. When the second semester began, all the students were moved into private homes with different families. Two students including myself were sent to a house that was owned by an elderly woman.

She laid down the rules at her house. We had to stay in our rooms; we weren't allowed downstairs, not even for a drink of water; we each had a glass and had to get our drinking water from the tap in the bathroom. She was not very friendly with us. I think taking us in was just another source of income for her.

As time passed, things got worse, to the point that I quit the program and went back home, even though I was in my second year of a two-year program. I was disappointed not to have completed the program, but I felt like being in a prison in her boarding house.

After returning home, I didn't want to go back working in the woods for private companies under contract with Bowater's.

On Labour Day weekend, my friends William Alley and Robert Shears and I were in an accident on the Trans-Canada Highway in the Codroy Valley. Robert's girlfriend, Florence Pretty, was teaching in Port-Aux-Basque, so we drove her out there from St. David's. We were in a Volkswagen Beatle, a small car that was totally demolished in the crash.

On the way back home, late at night, I was sitting in the front seat, and my friend William was driving; Robert was sitting in the back seat. I saw a car coming towards us and didn't give it much thought. Then, with no warning, it ran into us head on. We went off the highway and rolled over down a steep bank. The car hit large boulders as it started to roll and landed on its roof. The other car went on the other side of the highway but did not roll over.

Robert got thrown out through the back windshield, William also was thrown out through the door when it opened on impact. I braced myself and held on to the hand grip that was on the dashboard in the car. When the car came to a stop, it was bottom-up resting on its roof, and I could not get out. The dash was crushed by the boulders and my hand was stuck in the grip. I didn't know if I was seriously hurt or not at that time.

William and Robert came to the car and assisted me in getting out. Robert had a broken collarbone, while William had damage to both of his kneecaps. He could barely stand up.

We finally got back on the highway and went on the other side to the other vehicle that ran into us. There were four people in the other car who were injured and needed medical attention.

We were in total darkness but managed to get everyone back on the highway and wait for a car to come by and assist us.

At last, another car came by. One of its passengers was a nurse. She checked out the people who were injured and knew they needed to go to the hospital in Port-Aux-Basque. They made room in their car for everyone except me, since it appeared that I wasn't seriously injured. I felt okay with just a few bruises and scratches, so they left me on the highway alone. I waited in total darkness for a car to come by so I could get a ride home.

Finally, Mackey Gillis, a man from the Highlands, drove by and gave me a ride home to St. David's. It was quite an experience to say the least. I was shaken up after I realized how serious it could have been. When word got around about the accident, people didn't know that I was also in the car.

William had to have surgery to repair the damage to his kneecaps. He and Robert were in the Port-Aux-Basque hospital for a week or more before being released. It was months before they went back to work with Bowater's cutting and hauling pulp wood.

Chapter 3 - My Electrifying Career (and Music and Love)

My close friend Ulric was working at his father's electrical company, doing interior wiring in communities as electricity came to them. (A lot of communities had no electricity back in the 1960s.) They hired me as an apprentice and trained me in interior wiring.

I enjoyed working for and with them, I started when they were wiring houses in Burnt Islands, Rose Blanche and Harbour le Cou. We finished work in that area and moved to South Brook and Robert's Arm area. We were there for several months as only a limited number of private companies were doing interior wiring.

After finishing in that area, we started on the Northern Peninsula – Trout River and Bonne Bay – canvassing the community for houses to wire. The first house we wired in

Trout River was Walter Harris' residence; that is where I met my future wife, Katie. She was not quite sixteen at the time, but she was very mature and looked older. She was a beautiful young woman.

We boarded at Fred Barnes' residence in Trout River. There were also two female teachers staying there; it was their first-year teaching. They both married men from Trout River, after their first year there.

After we finished wiring Katie's father's house, we started dating and enjoyed being together. People in the community were undecided about getting their houses wired as they didn't think the government would bring electricity to their region. We completed around ten to fifteen houses, then decided to move down the northern coast where communities were waiting for wiring. We left Trout River and moved our operation to Brig Bay where we had a list of houses to install interior wiring.

In those days, there were not many clubs

and bars on the Northern Peninsula. In Plum Point, close to Brig Bay, Ike Gibbons had a bar with a dance floor for young people and it was filled every weekend when a band played.

There were no musical bands in the area back then. The Gosse family was very musical, so we decided to start a band and play at the club on the weekends. A group of young people in the town of Robinsons had a band. When they had a disagreement and split up, they agreed to sell their equipment to us. I bought the drums and two microphones. Rodney bought the amplifier and the other basic equipment we needed. Ulric was the rhythm guitar player and the vocalist, while Rodney was the drummer. Ulric's Brother, Derrick, played lead guitar. I was the so-called manager, who was responsible for collecting the money at the door. We decided to name the band the Hurricanes.

We were the first band on the Northern Peninsula, and it was a hit from the first week. The young people loved it, since it was new to their area. The owner was happy, as his club was packed on every weekend and he did great business selling alcohol and beer. Every weekend, the Hurricanes played at the club, with the dance floor at full capacity. The club owner's father was the mayor of Brig Bay and, being a consumer of alcohol, was excited when we were at his son's club.

At that time, the roads down the Northern Peninsula were gravel. When we went back and forth, it took us two days to get from Deer Lake to Brig Bay. Because the roads were so muddy and rough, we decided not to take our equipment there some weeks. Ike Gibbons was disappointed and offered to go to St. David's and get it, so he would have a band to play on the weekends.

It was a good experience for us all. We worked doing interior wiring during the week and entertained at the club on the weekend. Of course, we single guys were a hit with the young gals who really enjoyed the band. For a while I dated Irene Coles from Savage Cove who was teaching in Brig Bay. I also dated a young lady, Bernadette Hoddinott, from Brig Bay, nothing serious just like close friends.

We finally finished wiring houses and decided to move elsewhere. We went back to Trout River to wire more houses that wanted our service and that gave me an opportunity to connect with Katie again.

After we moved out of the area, Katie and I saw less of each other and decided to go our separate ways. I knew it was more difficult for her than me. She was only fifteen when I met her, but she was very mature for her age.

I started dating a girl from Robinsons, named Laura Morris, who also was a teenager. We connected because her mom had passed away when she was a child, and my father passed away when I was young. I think that brought us closer to each other. She was a beautiful young woman, that I was proud to be with. We dated for around six months, then she told me she was pregnant and wanted to know what we were going to do. I was unemployed, had no income and felt helpless because I knew she wanted to get married. If I had had a steady job, I would have happily married her. I suggested that we wait a while, and hopefully things would change regarding my situation. I didn't want to get married and live on welfare.

It was difficult for me to see her as we were living in different communities that were miles apart. I had to depend on others to get a ride to Robinsons to see her. About a week after she told me she was pregnant, I called her at her sister's home, where she was living. When I asked to speak to Laura, they said she wasn't there. I tried several times to talk with her on the phone but did not get any answer from her sister. It was like she had disappeared, and I didn't know where she was.

Months later, I heard from a friend that Laura's sister shipped her off to Mary's Harbour in Labrador. I never saw her or had any contact with her after that. I heard through her sister-in-law that she married a man in Mary's Harbour, so I assumed she was okay and didn't want any contact with me.

I didn't know for a long time that she gave birth to a boy. I didn't know his name and felt like no one cared, seeing as she was married and going on with her life. It was always on my mind that I had a son out there who probably hated me, and that was not a good feeling.

I decided to get on with my life. With no work in St. David's, I applied to the Canadian Armed Forces.

Father Dan LaFrance, Katie and me. Father Dan was the Catholic chaplain, a personal friend.

Chapter 4 – My Years in Uniform

I received a letter to report to the service-recruiting centre in St. John's to go through the medical and aptitude testing process. I passed all the tests and was screened to join the Canadian Engineers. I was proud of that as my brother Cas was also an engineer who had served in the same corps.

The day I was going to be sworn in, the officer asked me if I had anything to declare. I was confused by not knowing what he was getting at. He told me Laura's sister had contacted them, informing them I was running away from my responsibility for her sister's child.

I didn't know Laura had a son. I asked the officer, "What do I need to do?" He told me I would have to go home, contact the welfare officer in Stephenville, and sign a document to financially support her child. That is what I did without any hesitation, as I knew in the forces I would have a steady income, so it was a non-issue. I immediately went to Stephenville as soon as I got back home and signed the required documents.

A week later I received word from the recruiting office to return to St. John's for further instructions and take the oath of allegiance to Canada. I was still concerned about Laura and my son, whom I found out later was named Michael. I was still bothered by the fact that I had a son that I probably would never see, and who probably hated his father, thinking I had abandoned him and his mother. It was not a good feeling, but at least I could pay child support that would help them.

I left St. John's and had to report to the army base in Halifax for further testing, which was the standard procedure before going to an army training centre.

Along the way, I met three other guys

from Newfoundland who were also accepted for training in the Royal Canadian Engineer Corps. We were sent to Calgary for basic training at the Queen's Own Rifles infantry base. Due to the slow recruiting process, we had to wait until we had several recruits screened before our basic training started.

Back then, the training was tough. Before we graduated, our unit went from thirty-six men to around twenty-seven. Some were sent back for more training, and some were dismissed and sent home. I was the oldest soldier in the group, at the age of twenty-one.

Our original group of thirty-six recruits at the start of training for the Royal Canadian Engineering Corps in Calgary.

Our sergeant was of German nationality; Sergeant Muller required the best of every soldier. He wanted the 155 Platoon to be the best, so everything had to be immaculate, and perfect. Upon graduation, a soldier was chosen as the best recruit in the platoon, but that wasn't something we tried as soldiers to achieve.

Being tall, I was given the position of right marker in the platoon; it was a difficult position as every step, turn, and drill movement was based on the right marker. I assumed that I would only fill the role for a while and Sergeant Muller would later select someone else.

After weeks of drill training, I knew I was stuck with this position. No one had any idea who he would select for the best recruit. That person would have his name engraved on a large trophy, which would be placed in the Military Museum, and given a silver stein with his name on it to signify the honour.

There I am, front row on the far left with my graduating class of 27 men.

Graduation day came and we were all excited that we made it through basic training and would go to our specified field for training in the corps. We all assembled on the parade square and were put through all the paces of the different drill movements. Everything was done in uniformity, with no room for mistakes. As the right marker I was pleased that everything was executed, as Sergeant Muller would say, "immaculately."

Finally, it was time to announce the best recruit in our platoon. I was surprised when he called out my name – Sapper King. I then broke rank and marched out to receive the trophy, which was presented by the base commander, Colonel Swan.

It was a day of celebration for us, as our team of soldiers were like brothers. In our platoon, there were Queen's Own Rifles, Provost Corps, RCEME, Royal Canadian Engineers, etc. But we were all one team during training.

Salvation Army uniform / military uniform, Royal Canadian Engineers.

The engineer school for further training was in Chilliwack BC, at Veeder Crossing, That was the training centre for the Royal Canadian Engineers, where we trained in explosives, bridge building, planting and clearing mine fields, and water purification. On our last exercise out in the bush, we were doing a mock battle with civilian men acting as the enemy. We were shooting back and forth at each other with blank ammunition. One of the civilians shouted out, "I am shot" and we thought he was just trying to make it sound real, until he shouted it out the second time.

Then everything stopped. We realized that he had been hit in the stomach by two bullets. The exercise was cancelled, and they started an internal investigation. Our troop was interrogated. They assumed that someone had put real bullets intentionally in their magazine with the blanks. We were to go on leave after this exercise, but that also was cancelled. Eventually, they found out the blank and real ammunitions were manufactured by the same company. Live rounds had been mixed with the blanks by mistake. We graduated and my friend Ron Bannister received the award for the best recruit in the unit.

Two months after the investigation was complete, we were transferred to our unit in CFB Gagetown, New Brunswick, and assigned to the two-field squadron of the Royal Canadian Engineers. I was still unsettled about what happen to Laura and my son Mike. I started drinking heavily and didn't focus a lot on the military. Alcohol was cheap in the military. Every base had its own bar, called the Wets. Every weekend, we had a Happy Hour, when you could buy beer for a cent a glass.

I had good buddies, Wesley Halfyard and Ron Bannister and James Dennis, who looked out for me. We are still friends today more than fifty years later.

Me and Jim Dennis were good friends and became drinking buddies. Jim was originally from Corner brook. It was normal for soldiers to drink as the alcohol was cheap.

Before I enlisted in the military I had met a beautiful young lady in Trout River, Katie Harris. Katie was the youngest daughter of Walter and Elsie Harris, Walter and Elsie had five children, Elyard, Clyde, Eudora, Berta and Katie. Before I joined the military Katie and I went our different ways. Katie was raised in a very devout Christian family, that was closely connected to their church, The Salvation Army.

I remember the first time I saw her; we were in Trout River with Gosse Electric completing residential interior wiring before the electricity came to that area. Her family home was the first house we wired before they received electricity.

I started to reflect on my life and knew I needed to make some major changes and settle down and look to the future. I wrote a letter to Katie, who was still living in Trout River, to see if she wanted to connect and start a life together, I was tired of all the drinking and beating around I did. I got no response from her but decided to write a couple more letters before I stopped trying to contact her. After the fourth or fifth letter, I got a letter back from her saying she was interested in getting together, even though we had gone our separate ways.

Before I wrote her the first letter, I had done some internal processing to decide who I wanted to start a life with. I knew that she was the one and was very happy when she answered my letters. I found out later she didn't get my first three letters because she was in Corner Brook and her mother got her mail. When she saw the military emblem on the envelopes, she knew they were from me and destroyed the letters.

One weekend, Katie decided to go home to visit her parents. She asked her mother if anyone had picked up the mail that day, and her mother said, "No, not yet."

Katie went to the post office and received my fourth letter. She was excited to hear from me and wanted to be a part of my future plans.

Her parents were concerned as they didn't know me, and thought I was from Port-aux-Port, where people were referred to as Aboriginals; back then they were regarded as Jackos/Indians/etc.

I wanted to be honest with her, so I shared with her that I had a son with Laura, who was married and living in Labrador, raising Mike as their child. I wanted her to know that before I asked her to marry me. I didn't want any hidden agenda that she would be disappointed later when we were back together.

We were excited and happy to be with each other. I was on leave from December until mid-January and visited her in Trout River. It was exciting to be with her again, even though she was only seventeen and I was twenty-two. We talked about our new plans for our future. After I went back to CFB Gagetown, we wrote to each other almost every day, with the hope of being together forever.

In March, she told me she was pregnant and wanted to know what we were going to do. We made plans to get married when I came home on leave in July 1968.

I knew she didn't want to leave Newfoundland and go to Gagetown. She was having problems with her health, so we decided to put the move on the back burner for now. Her doctor tried to convince her to abort our baby. We were totally against her having an abortion, but he insisted that her life might be in danger due to the complications she was having with her pregnancy. She refused and continued on, even though she was not well at times.

A nurse in Trout River, who was an English woman, told Katie she would be there for her and to call on her anytime. Katie would have to go to the hospital a couple of times each month at Norris Point, which was a couple of hours away. Each time, the doctor told her that she should abort the baby for her own health.

Katie was a Salvation Army parishioner from birth and Christian principles were very important to her. She refused to take his advice, believing that everything would be fine.

Before I went home on leave in July, we were assigned to a special project in Sorel, Quebec. It was classified as top secret. The government had built a new submarine destroyer that was designed like a plane on the inside. It was constructed out of aluminium, a quarter-inch thick, and named the Hydrofoil 400. Our responsibility was to dismantle the project piece by piece and prepare if for shipping to Halifax, Nova Scotia for launching and testing.

It wasn't successful, as the Atlantic Ocean is rough and difficult to navigate in storms. They could not get it up on its foils in the rough seas. If you run a Google search for the Hydrofoil 400, you can see pictures of it in Bras d'Or, on display as a tourist attraction. You can visit the HCMS Bras d'Or and tour the interior of the ship. We were in Sorel for a month as engineers from the 2 Field Squadron.

We also did special training as a riot squad during the FLQ (October) crisis in Quebec. It was a very intensive training period, to shut down riots if needed. We were on standby for weeks, however we never got called to handle the riots in Quebec.

Our Blessed Wedding Day

I was on leave in July, and we got married in the Salvation Army church on July 26, 1968. We had our reception at the community centre in Trout River. The whole community was invited to our wedding. I wore a Royal Blue Uniform, for the Royal Canadian Engineers. It was a ceremonial uniform used for special occasions with a red stripe from the waist to the cuff on each leg. Katie wore a beautiful white wedding dress. She looked beautiful, and I was so proud to have her as my soulmate.

Bill Parson stood in as the father giver, as

Katie's father Walter was not comfortable doing it. Eudora and Berta were the bride's maids, and Elyard and Wilson were the bride boys..

We didn't make any plans for music at the reception, but unbeknownst to us, The Hurricanes came and played at our wedding reception. It was the best gift we received from Rodney, my stepbrother and his wife Edith, Ulric and his wife Marjorie, and Derrick.

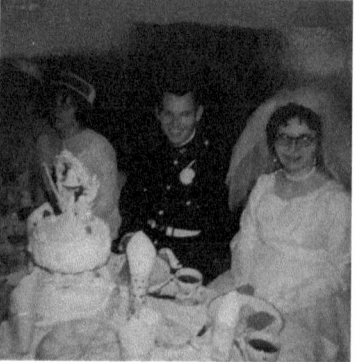

Two very happy newlyweds and their families in Trout River in 1968.

It was an exciting time for Katie and me, even though there were times she didn't feel well. It was a great celebration. We were married by a young lieutenant, Guy Roberts, who was stationed as the corps officer in Trout River.

Shortly afterward, my leave was over, and I had to return to CFB Gagetown in Oromocto. I applied for a permanent married quarters (PMQ) for us to live on the base or in an apartment downtown. On August 24, 1968, I received a call from Katie, announcing that we had a baby daughter. With all the complications she had had with her health, she had given birth prematurely at six months.

Our daughter weighed only two pounds and six ounces. The doctors and medical staff at the hospital in Corner Brook didn't think she would survive once she started to lose weight. The only equipment they had at the hospital were incubators, no modern technology like we have today.

They would not release our daughter until she weighed five pounds. She was in the hospital for three months before Katie could take her home. Even then, they were uncertain if she would make it. There were some health concerns since she was what we called a colic baby and needed special care. I was back at base camp and could not be there with Katie at this difficult time. With the help and care of Katie's mother, Elsie, they took turns around the clock caring for her, trying a lot of home remedies.

We had to put the idea for them moving to Oromocto on hold. Katie didn't really want to leave the security of being home with her parents who were there for her when she needed their help.

She encouraged me to get released from the military and come home where I was needed. At the same time, the government brought in unification, which changed everything in the forces. All units were classed as regular military services, with no more royal units. The government did not consult with the troops before they made these changes. All personnel were told that if they didn't agree with unification, they could apply for an honourable release. Thousands of soldiers disagreed with what the government did with the military and things started to go downhill.

Katie wanted me to get released and come home, even though I had no work in sight to make a living for us. She stressed the fact that we could live with her parents until we got settled. I was apprehensive, as I wanted to work and support my family and not depend on welfare assistance.

She indicated I could fish with her father

until something else came along. I had mixed feeling about going back with no concrete plans for guaranteed work.

After we discussed it in length, I decided to apply for an honourable release and focus on my family responsibility. It took me three months before everything came together and I got my discharge papers.

Chapter 5 – Finding Salvation with My Family

I was excited about going home to see my wife Katie and our daughter Yvette. I flew from the Fredericton airport to Stephenville on Dec 10, 1968. My brother-in-law Bill Parsons picked me up at the airport. It was a great feeling to know that soon I would see my daughter for the first time. It was so exciting to hold her in my arms for the first time. She was so small that I was scared that I might drop her.

It was a happy homecoming for me, even though employment was a big question mark. We discussed fishing with her father, Walter. This would be a new experience for me, and I really didn't want to fish for a living. Walter usually fished with a small number of lobster pots and a salmon trap. We would have to increase the number of lobster pots for both of us to make a living, I knew it would be a challenge.

We decided to make another one hundred and fifty lobster pots before the lobster season opened, bringing the total number to three hundred. Walter had his own sawmill by his garage so we started sawing lobster laths and cells that were needed to make the pots. It was a totally new learning experience for me, but I knew I needed to give it one hundred percent.

By the end of March, we had three hundred lobster pots ready for the water.

Our daughter Yvette's health was improving each day. It was exciting to be home with my family, taking care of them.

The other concern we had was that Walter had a back problem and could not haul a lot of lobster pots. I made it my responsibility to haul the three hundred pots each day and he would be responsible for operation of the outboard motor only. This was a challenge from the start. I had blisters on my hands from the rope, but I kept on doing it each day.

Fishing on the Atlantic Ocean outside of Trout River was tough. We were out in the Atlantic Ocean, with no bay or harbour to run into when a storm came our way. There were days when the sea was rough, as waves from the swell rose up to ten to twelve feet. If the waves started to break, we would head for shore. When we entered the cove, waves would be breaking across the beach. We were only in an open speed boat that was about sixteen feet long and sat low in the water. Walter would circle in the cove until the waves broke on the beach and watch for the next wave and ride it ashore like on a surfboard, projecting us upon the beach, completely out of the water.

It was scary for me at times, but I trusted Walter and knew he wouldn't take any unnecessary chances, being a fisherman for all his life. That summer we did well fishing together, but I knew it wasn't for me.

On February 13th 1970, we were blessed with another daughter, Michelle. She didn't have any health issues when she was born. I was the proud father of two beautiful daughters.

My mother-in-law, Elsie, often encouraged me to attend church at the Salvation Army. The last week of May, they were celebrating their Corps Anniversary. They had special guests from the headquarters in St. John's. I knew Katie wanted to go, as she had been very active in the Salvation Army as a young person and wanted to get involved again. I grew up in the Anglican Church and I didn't know much about the Salvation Army and its doctrine. I was confirmed in the Anglican church, and always considered myself Anglican.

My grandfather Tomas Taylor, my mother's father was a lay reader in the Anglican church in Morrisville.

My grandmother Charity Taylor was a very dedicated Christian woman. She had a profound impact on my life when I made a spiritual commitment to ministry.

I found the Salvation Army had a strange

way of worship in their service compared to the Anglican church.

I started my spiritual journey with the Salvation Army and always incorporated my Anglican theology in my new found faith.

I always had respect for other religions and treated people accordingly.

We went to the service with our two girls and sat in the back of the church, It was a very lively and spiritual service. After the message was delivered, the pastor invited people to come forward to make a spiritual commitment. Katie went forward to the mercy seat; I knew she would, as she wanted to commit her life to Christ.

There were sixty-plus people who went forward for salvation. I was sitting in the back with my two girls on my knees, waiting for Katie to come back so we could take them home. Out of curiosity, I looked around and saw the corps officer's wife, Bonnie, looking down with a smile on her face. I knew she was thinking of

Katie and me.

I didn't know what happened next. There I was weeping and didn't know what was happening to me; I literally ran and knelt at the altar by my wife as we both committed our lives spiritually to the Lord. Afterward, I was confused as I didn't really understand what it was all about. I grew up in the Anglican faith and this was a new experience for me.

I felt that we had also made a new commitment to our marriage relationship, sealed with our spiritual commitment. First thing I did when I got home was pour six beers, that I had for the weekend, down the sink. I never ever had a struggle with alcohol that I couldn't control, but had other vices to deal with.

I had many struggles with smoking and foul language. I knew it had to change. I smoked two packs of cigarettes a day and was totally addicted. I remember one day after making a commitment to change, Walter and I launched our boat to go fishing when the motor wouldn't start. I started swearing. Walter didn't say anything. I knew that I messed up and thought my spiritual commitment was over.

When we came back to the beach with our catch for the day, I saw Lieutenant Bussey waiting for us to dock. I was embarrassed to see him. I told him what happened and that I thought I had lost out and was no longer serving the Lord. He was very understanding and told me that I need to confess it to the Lord and pray about it. He said, "This is a habit you had for years, and it will take time to get beyond it." He told me to keep trusting in the Lord and growing in my faith. It was the best news I had received all week.

A month after we dedicated our lives to God's service, the corps officers, Lieutenants Lester and Bonnie Bussey, were appointed to another corps. Captains Fred and Shirley Ash came to Trout River as the new pastors.

When the new captains started their ministry in Trout River, we looked to them for spiritual direction and guidance in newfound faith. They were very understanding and patient with us as we stumbled along each day on our spiritual journey. Fred and Shirley ministered to us and kept encouraging us each day with the struggles we were facing.

Katie always wanted to be involved in Ministry, even at a young age. We not only made a spiritual commitment but committed our lives to each other in our relationship. Our whole family life changed with our spiritual commitment. We were closer together as a family. We were excited and decided to build a house for our family. Her father Walter had a sawmill. I started cutting logs for the lumber we needed. It was long tiring days, fishing each day, and in the woods cutting logs after docking our boat.

It was hard work but very rewarding when we saw our house being built. It was my first attempt at building a house and I made a lot of mistakes along the way.

However, we didn't live in our house very long, as I got transferred to Rocky Harbour, working on the Gros Morn National Park. Realizing that we wouldn't move back to Trout River we sold our house before we went into the ministry.

Chapter 6 - Blazing New Trails

After the fishing season was over, I decided to pursue other avenues for employment. I applied for upgrading in Stephenville and was accepted. I stayed in the old military barracks that had been abandoned by the Americans. I would come home every weekend with Gary Crocker and his friend from Trout River. I knew Katie did not like the idea of me being away as she wanted me home with her, Yvette, and Michelle. However, I wanted to upgrade my education so that I could support my family.

At that time, there were rumours of the creation of a new National Park that would employ a lot of people. Out of curiosity, I got an application from Manpower, as it was called then and applied for a position as a foreman on the park.

I really wasn't convinced that the park would be established in our area. I went back to Stephenville to continue my education after the weekend was over. Mid-week, I received a call from Katie, telling me I had an interview in Rocky Harbour for employment on the park, and she wanted me to quit and come home. I wasn't sure if it was just to get me home, so I questioned it. Walter came on the phone to confirm that I had a letter about an interview for a job on the park, so I knew it had to be real.

That weekend, I came home and prepared for the interview. I met with staff in Rocky Harbour for the interview and was encouraged about having a job on the park.

A week or two after the interview, I got a letter saying that I had the position of foreman and would be supervising ten men to cut the park boundary around Trout River and up the head of Trout River Pond. It was exciting knowing that I had a job on the park and didn't have to move away.

We started cutting the park boundary line in November. It was great to have guaranteed weekly employment with a decent salary. We cut the boundary line around Trout River to the head of Trout River Pond. I had a great crew of men working with me from Trout River: Sam Snook, Walter Snook, Sandy Snook, Bill Hann, George Crocker, and Leonard White . We never missed a day's work all winter.

We worked for five months then we were laid off. The Shear family in Rocky Harbour was upset because the government would not pay them what they wanted for their land. The government was going to expropriate the land for what is now known as Gros Morne Park. There was a lot of uncertainty if the park would go ahead or not since Prime Minister Pierre Trudeau was undecided about signing off on it.

Being out of work, and not wanting to go back to fishing, was very frustrating for those of us who wanted to work on the park. Before the fishing season started in April, I got a call from the park office in Rocky Harbour, informing me that the five of the men who worked on the boundary line were invited to work as a maintenance crew until the land issue was resolved.

We moved from Trout River to Rocky Harbour in April, and I started work on the park again. We rented Irene Decker's mother's house and tried to settle in.

This move, even though it was not far from Trout River, was very difficult for Katie. She felt more secure living close by her parents.

I made a commitment to her that we would go back home every weekend. We had our own house there that we finished when I worked on the base line with my crew in Trout River. We completed our house but never had an opportunity to settle in and enjoy it. We came home on the weekends to visit Katie's family and spent the rest of our time in Rocky Harbour.

The park superintendent for the first year

was Mr. Dollimount. When he retired, a young man named James Vollmershausen replaced him. The general manager was Derm Russell. Freeman Timmons was the chief warden. These three were the managing team who made all the decisions regarding the park.

There still was a lot of unrest in the community over the land issue. Finally in May 1971, the Trudeau government signed off on the land and gave $5 million for park development. As foremen on the last project, I was excited to know that we would be back with a crew to help build the park.

On the first project, Ted Shears was the general foreman who supervised all the crews and foremen. We had wondered if he would be back after all the delays. We were told that the park was going to hire around a hundred men and start developing, trails, campgrounds, picnic areas, and special sights along the coast.

We were all excited about a secure job with the federal government and about the park becoming a reality. We were ready to go and wondered what our project would be now that everything was resolved.

While we were waiting and working away as a maintenance team, the custodian Richard Pittman informed me that I had an interview with the management team. I assumed he was playing a trick on me and refused to go to the office. Shortly afterward, he came back in the staff car and told me they were waiting, and I needed to go to the office. It was coffee time, around 10 a.m. so I went back with him.

When I went into the office, I was told to go into the boardroom. To my surprise, the superintendent, general manager and the chief warden were there waiting for me. They were interviewing for a new general foreman to supervise and be responsible for all the crews. I was confused because I did not apply for the general foreman's position; I thought I would be a foreman with my own crew. I sat there for about twenty minutes, answering their questions then the general manager told me to go for my coffee break.

Before I finished my coffee break, Derm called me outside in the yard and told me to go and change the colour of my hard hat as I was his new general foreman. What a surprise that was! I had no idea this was coming but was excited with this promotion.

He told me that they were hiring around a hundred men, so I needed to get busy purchasing tools and equipment for each crew. We had to purchase a lot of equipment, including pickup trucks and vans to transport the crews to their worksites. I set up an office in the compound area that was built for the surveyors. It was very exciting starting out in an unexpected new position.

I later learned that Derm didn't want to hire Ted Shears for the job, because of the trouble the Shears made over the land issue. Derm and I had served in the military, we got along great and had a lot in common. He depended on me to supervise the projects my crews were working on. We had a good working relationship, and he realized that he could depend on me to get things done. We were a team, and all the work crews were hard working men, who appreciated having a job. They were the hardest and best workers I ever knew.

I had been the union representative for the men, and they decided to call a meeting, as I now was a part of management. They wanted a new person to represent them. That was okay with me as I had other responsibilities that kept me busy. In a meeting with Derm, he informed me not to buy any materials for the park from the Shears. They owned most of the businesses in Rocky Harbour, including the lumber yards, garages, gas pumps, etc.

    Roland Pittman in Norris Point had a limited lumberyard, where I purchased all the lumber we needed for the walking trails going to

Western Brook Pond and other projects. If he didn't have it on hand, he would order it for me. That worked out great and it increased his business which greatly pleased him.

I then went to Dave Pittman, who had opened a garage to repair vehicles in Rocky Harbour. He also had gas pumps to supply our vehicles with fuel. He was pleased with this new arrangement, as he had assumed all the park business for supplies would go to the Shears. That had all changed after the land dispute.

Each foreman was assigned to a project with their crew. One crew was building the boardwalk into Western Brook Pond. Another crew was working on the trail up Gros Morne Mountain, while other crews were clearing campsites at Berry Hill, Kill Devil Mountain, and Western Brook. We had a carpentry crew building a small shelter and storage units for emergency supplies at the head of Western Brook Pond. They also built a small dory that would be used in case of emergency at the head of the pond if someone got stranded.

Parks Canada rented a helicopter from the Viking Helicopter company in Deer Lake to take material, sections of cabins, and other supplies to the interior of the park. One day, they decided to take the dory to the head of Western Brook Pond. They opened both doors and loaded the dory into the helicopter with each end overhanging outside the chopper.

Fralin Cullihall and I sat in the dory to keep it balanced during the flight. The pilot and the chief warden Freeman Timmons were seated up front. They were having trouble with the engine. It kept backfiring and sputtering out black smoke. Needless to say, this made me very nervous. I was not excited about flying and, with the engine trouble, I determined that this would be my last trip with Viking. It was quite an experience for us all. However, everything went okay and we returned to the compound safely. Afterward I used to joke that I flew over the mountains in a dory.

The first year was a challenge for me, being the general foreman over all the projects we were working on. I would write a report each weekend, summarizing what each crew had completed at each site and what foreman was responsible for overseeing each project.

The following year, Derm informed me he was being transferred to the head office in St. John's. Before he left, he encouraged Warren Smith to take his position as general manager of the park.

Warren was working for the Department of Highways as a manager of projects in our area. This was a new position for him with the Gros Morne National Park, and Derm told me that he would be depending on me to be his right-hand man. He informed me that Warren would need all the update information on each project until he got settled into his new position on the park. I started working with Warren and provided him with all the information he needed. We developed a good relationship working together.

I informed Warren that I had committed myself to ministry with the Salvation Army and I would attend college for two years in St. John's before I was ordained and commissioned. Apparently, it must have slipped his mind.

Around June, he informed me that a new position was coming on stream as the supervisor for operations on the Gros Morne Park. He wanted me to take this new role and continue as his right-hand man.

I reminded him again about my plans for ministry and the commitment I made before I came to work on the park. I told him I appreciated his offer, but I needed to fill my commitment to ministry. I told him I would resign my position in August and take a month's vacation before I moved to St. John's for training. I sensed he was disappointed because he thought I would take this new job. This also confirmed to me that he appreciated my work as his general foreman.

During my work on the park in Rocky Harbour Katie and I were faced with a challenge before we could be accepted into the ministry. We had to finish our high school education . We were discouraged as this seemed impossible at our age, with a family. We talked to our pastors Captains Fred and Shirley Ash, and Fred threw out a challenge to us. He said we could complete our high school education through the mail from an educational college in Toronto if we were really committed to the ministry. Katie and I knew this would be a major goal for us to achieve, but we were determined and gave it our best We applied for the correspondence courses we need, and stared studying weekly. After two years plus we received our diplomas and was accepted as candidates for the next session at The Salvation Army College for Officer Training in St. John's. We received a lot of help and support from Shirley and Fred as we struggled with our lessons. Captain Fred was not only the pastor for the Salvation Army in the community but also taught in the elementary school daily.

Without his and Shirley's help and encouragement we would have gotten discouraged and quit. They were a pastor team who loved the people they ministered to daily. I said, to Fred and Shirley after we were commissioned as officers, that they were very brave people to support and back us for the ministry. We have been close friends over the years and shared a lot of special gatherings together and much laughter.

On August 1, 1974, I left Rocky Harbour with my family to get ready for our new adventure at The Salvation Army College for Officer Training in St. John's. We sold our house to help us financially, as we had to have enough funds to last for two years while we both were in college. This was another challenge for Katie as she didn't want to be away from her family in Trout River. This was a huge challenge for us as a family, as it would impact our daughters as well. It was a difficult two years of training, with two children. There were times we struggled with assignments especially with the responsibility of a family. We gave it our all, and left everything with the Lord.

We were in St John's for two years before we were ordained/commissioned as Salvation Army officers. The name of our session of cadets was The Overcomers. The second year of training we found out that Katie was pregnant. The Salvation Army regulations at the time stated that cadets had to leave training for a year if they were having a child.

We contacted Major Eric Brown and gave him the news about our situation, I told him that if we had to leave college, we would not be back. I was thirty years old at the time and could not put our lives on hold for another year.

He contacted the training principal, Major Herb Snelgrove, who advised us that they would work things out for us. We appreciated their support and continued on with our training. March 25th, 1976, we were blessed with another beautiful daughter, Rochelle Barbara King. Even with her pregnancy and family duties, Katie missed fewer classes than the single girls did. Rochelle was three months old when we were ordained/commissioned by General Arnold Brown. She was the youngest Overcomer in our session.

Two years at the training college was difficult for us as a family, especially at our age. We were closely supervised and had to get permission for the least little things pertaining to our personal life. We weren't allowed to own a car, or even a television. That was difficult as Katie always enjoyed watching children's programs with our girls.

Chapter 7 - Our First Salvation Army Appointments

Our first appointment was to Ming's Bight, as their corps officers. I didn't know where it was located since this was the first time I had heard of it. We moved to the north shore community on June 23rd, 1976, with our three daughters, Yvette, Michelle and Rochelle. Yvette was seven years old, Michelle was five and a half and Rochelle was four months old.

Despite our excitement to be pastors in Ming's Bight, there was a lot of uncertainly because the residence was for a single minister, and it was not suitable or large enough for a family of five. I met with the people around August to discuss our situation and to encourage them to build a new home that would accommodate our family.

They were very receptive about the ideas we presented to them and appreciated that we were the first married couple with children appointed as their pastors. A group of men volunteered to cut logs during the winter for lumber that was needed to build the new house. Each day, I would go in the woods with the men and work with them.

That winter, we had more than a thousand logs ready for the sawmill in LaScie. Gid Sacrey, the owner of the mill, offered to saw the logs into lumber. Half would go to the mill and half would go to us for the quarters, with no money being exchanged.

We started building the residence around April 1977 and finished it in October, all completed by free labour. We moved in and furnished it with all new furniture, even a forced-air oil furnace. The old home had a floor furnace that was fuelled by gravity flow with no ducts, only the main grate above the furnace.

During this time, we continued to visit our people weekly and held two worship services each Sunday When we were building the new quarters, Katie and I worked as a team building the quarters and in ministry. We had a successful spiritual ministry. Several men made spiritual commitments that were life-changing for them. Some people came back to church after being away for years.

In May 1978, we received word from the Salvation Army Headquarters in St. John's that we were being transferred to the Green's Harbour Corps in Trinity Bay. We were shocked by this news since we thought we would be in Ming's Bight for three to five years before moving. We had just built a new home and had moved in only seven months previously.

The Salvation Army decides how long officers stay in an appointment and people like us had no input into the decisions they made.

Being committed to ministry, we packed up our personal belongings for our new destination. During our ministry in Ming's Bight, we received a salary of $69 weekly. It was like a survival pay for a family of five. This amount would increase in small increments yearly.

This was totally different from the salary I had when working for the federal government at Gros Morne National Park. We knew our salary would be minimal, and it was not a major concern for us as we were committed to ministry to people not as a job for income alone.

We said our goodbyes to the people in Ming's Bight, after they held a social gathering in the community centre and shared a meal with us. It was sad leaving as it was our first appointment in ministry and we loved ministering to them as our people.

We arrived in Green's Harbour in the last week of June. The Salvation Army held a congress in the stadium in St. John's that weekend. Salvationists from all over Newfoundland gathered there for the weekend as most corps across the island were closed for this special weekend. The General of the Salvation Army was the guest speaker at all events. The General ordained and commissioned the new officers with the rank of lieutenant and appointed them to their designated corps in Newfoundland.

Everyone enjoyed these special events, and they gave us a time to relax and be ministered to by our General. It was exciting to attend congress and meet a lot of our colleagues and friends that we hadn't seen for a long time.

Before we went to congress, we visited our new quarters to check it out. It was a larger residence that would accommodate our family. The girls were excited that they each had their own bedrooms. We unpacked some of our personal belongings before we headed to St. John's.

I went to my office in the basement of the quarters, checked out the mail and looked at the financial statements pertaining to the Corps. I was surprised at what I found. They had a balance of $50 for the church expenses and zero for the young people's ministry. We were in a predicament. Our salary was $69 a week and there weren't enough funds to cover it. There was no church service during the congress weekend with no income for that week. It was frustrating to say the least. The fridge was empty, and we had nothing to feed the children.

I called the Divisional Commander, Brigadier Arthur Pike, and let him know the situation we were in. I thought he would give us support and help us with the predicament. I asked him if we could use the $50 for food, so our children had something to eat. He said no, that was for the Red Shield Program and could only be used for people on welfare who needed assistance in the community. I was upset with his response. Before we finished our conversation, he said point blank, "You have your work cut out for you." I was very disappointed in the lack of support I received from him and felt that he wasn't a very caring leader.

Being committed to ministry, we took it in good stride. After our first Sunday church services, the corps treasurer came to my office to do the accounting for the past week. She was aware of our situation and empathized with us. She wrote out cheques for all the bills outstanding for the week, with no funds left to pay our salary.

The Salvation Army had a policy that all bills had to be paid before officers received their salaries. We were short of funds and were going on vacation for three weeks with no compensation.

A kind soldier of the corps found out about our predicament, came to the residence and gave me $120. He encouraged us to take a vacation and said they would work something out when we got back.

It was greatly appreciated as we were tired from all the work, we had done in Ming's Bight, building the new quarters. We never had any financial difficulties there; they always had enough funds to cover our salary and all expenses for the corps bills.

Being interested in the property, I did a tour around the church and house, and was surprised at what I found. The church needed a lot of repairs. The siding was rotten. You could shove your fingers through it, and I knew it needed to be removed and new siding installed. I also found that most of the windows were rotten and need to be replaced. This would be a big challenge for me due to the lack of funds on hand.

At my first corps council meeting, I presented the members with the situation of their property. They realized that it needed to be repaired but were only concerned about the church. They thought the residence was good enough for us to live in. At that meeting, I brought to their attention that the federal government had a program for communities to apply for a project to give employment to people with little or no income. I told them we should apply so we could at least repair our church. They weren't interested and did not want to help me apply for it.

In my office, I decided to make up a proposal and submit it to the federal government. I made up a budget to cover the cost of materials and labour. I knew how much lumber was needed for this building project as I had experience in building when I worked on the Gros Morne Park. I decided that we should try to get a grant to build a youth hall on the church at the same time. The corps council didn't disagree with me, but they thought it was useless to try. I did up a construction budget of around $90,000 and would look after at the cost to do the inside later. The council thought it was a waste of time and didn't support me or help with my proposal.

I submitted the proposal to the Federal Government in October 1979 and waited for a response. Around the first week of January 1980, I received a call from the federal minister who was responsible for our area. He informed me that my proposal was accepted, and I would get a grant of $79,000 for my project and could hire ten men on this project. It would start around the first week of November 1981.

This was exciting news, knowing that when we started the youth centre attached to the church, we could do the repairs on the siding of the church and other necessary work. I held another meeting with the corps council and discussed the plans that I had sent to the government. They were surprised that I got the grant.

I went to St. John's to go over the details with our Divisional Commander, Colonel Albert Browning. I knew he would support this program. I told him that there were no funds available to repair the quarters, which was badly needed. He told me to go back, call another meeting and tell the people the quarters must be repaired. I knew the people on our board weren't interested in the condition of the quarters and their main concern was the church. He reiterated that I needed to have another meeting and let the people know.

The Salvation Army would give them a loan for $20,000 and they would only have to pay back $10,000 to the Army. I knew the board would not go for it, but I called the meeting and told them what the Army was offering them. They rejected it right away with little discussion or concern.

I went back to divisional headquarters, met with Colonel Browning, and told him about the results from my meeting with the corps council. He was not happy with them as he appreciated the work I was proposing to do on the quarters and citadel.

He told me to go back and set up another meeting with our board and Major Curt Keeping, his program director. Curt would come and talk to the people about the need to repair the quarters. I told him they would think that it was my idea and still refuse the Army's offer.

He told me point blank that he knew how hard we were working as their pastors, that if they refused to take out the loan of $20,000 with only having to pay half back, he would remove us from Green's Harbour and give us another appointment.

I appreciated his support and knew he was on my side regarding this issue. I set up another meeting, and Major Keeping came from headquarters to explain their offer. I opened the meeting and passed it over to him. He again explained about the loan and how they would benefit with this generous offer from the Army. I did not get involved in the discussion because I knew they thought it was my idea for him to come and try to convince them to accept. At first, they discussed it among themselves and said no to the suggested loan.

I was disappointed and felt let down by the board members who had no concern for their pastors' residence. Major Keeping laid out all the options and informed them by refusing this offer, it would be difficult for any projects needed in the corps. They again discussed his proposal and finally said yes to the loan. I knew that it wasn't because they wanted it; they were sort of put in a bind.

I was disappointed in the way they viewed this proposal. Here I had a grant from the federal government for $79,000 and another $20,000 the Army offered them for a total sum of $99,000. They only had to pay back $10,000 to the Army.

I opened a special account at the Bank of Montreal, which was the only bank in our area. We hired a foreman for the project and screened nine men for the labour that was needed. They worked from January until the last week of June, when the project was finished, as the first stage of the youth centre.

Chapter 8 – Entering the Field of Corrections

From 1980 until 1981, I applied for off-campus courses that were offered through Memorial University in St. John's. My first course was a second-year course in psychology. Although I had not done the first year, they accepted me as they needed enough students for the class, which was held at a satellite campus in Whitbourne.

It was a tough course, but I did pass the final test. That was my first experience with Memorial's studies. I then applied for the Correctional Program they were offering, as I had interest in ministering in prisons. This was a two-year course, and I knew it would be beneficial for me in the future.

I got permission from my Divisional Commander to do these studies and informed him

I would like to be involved in prison ministry. A month before our project ended, he phoned and said Katie and I were appointed to the Correctional Services of the Salvation Army in Edmonton, Alberta. I would be the executive director of this department and Katie would be the director of programs. I was excited as I realized hard work pays off. Again however, I knew this would be a struggle and challenge for Katie to leave Newfoundland and move so far away from her family.

She was receptive to this move, and at the end of June we left Green's Harbour on vacation before we left the island. We completed our vacation the end of July and started on our journey with our family to our new appointment in Edmonton.

It took us eight days to drive west. We made it into a travelling vacation for our family as our first time driving across Canada. While we were crossing the country, our appointment changed. The officer at the correctional services in Edmonton, Major George Barber, refused to move from his position and accept his new appointment.

When we arrived in Edmonton, we discovered that we were now appointed to the Edmonton Remand Centre, a provincial prison, as chaplains. We never questioned the change to accommodate Major Barber. It was disappointing, but we were dedicated to ministry, no matter what the appointment might have been.

When we went to our residence, we were shocked to find that the previous officers had literally wrecked the inside. They had been dismissed due to their personal conduct and they did not leave happily. It was an old house that needed a lot of repairs. There were holes in the walls everywhere. It was a mess. Again, we tried to settle into our new ministry.

It was very difficult with our living conditions in such a deplorable condition. We notified The Salvation Army Territorial Headquarters in Toronto and the response was slow. We knew they needed to buy a new home for our family.

Our beloved daughters Michelle, Rochelle and Yvette.

Katie and I always worked as a team. We started our ministry at the Remand Centre and were welcomed by the superintendent and staff. They made the transition for us easy. The only other chaplain was Father Daniel Lafrance, a Catholic priest. Dan was very accommodating and gave us a tour of the institution. The Remand Centre was the first electronic prison in Canada. With no bars on the units, every door was controlled electronically, even the elevators.

We were under the direction of the territory headquarters in Toronto and not connected to the divisional headquarters in Edmonton. We decided to worship at the Edmonton Temple. The pastors, Majors Ted and Phyllis Percy, were also from Newfoundland, so we had a lot in common. However, we had our own ministry at the Centre and conducted Sunday services for the inmates in the chapel.

Every year, the Salvation Army held a retreat for all officer personnel and retired officers. Our first retreat was in Banff, Alberta at the Red Carpet Inn and Conference Centre. It was a beautiful place to hold a retreat. The hot springs were across the street from the hotel. The retreat started on Friday and ended on Monday. It was a spiritual time for everyone and gave us the opportunity to meet all the Salvation Army officers in Alberta.

Major Herb Snelgrove was the Divisional Commander for Alberta and was concerned about our situation with the old quarters. Commissioner Waldron was on tour and going to the Yukon with him. He wanted permission to discuss our quarters with him. We said sure, we knew he had an interest in our ministry as Herb and Pearl were our training principals when we went through college. Shortly after, we got a response from THQ, regarding purchasing a new house. They agreed to purchase one and sell the old one later.

We kept informing the territory headquarters that they needed to purchase new property, to ensure that we had a decent house for our family. They finally decided to buy a new house, but they wanted the old one sold first. This was a problem because they wanted around $90,000 for the old one. People would come and look but had no interest due to the poor condition it was in.

Finally, they gave us permission to buy a new residence and the real estate would look after the old one at a reduced rate. We finally moved into a beautiful house that was close to our work and the church we would be attending. This helped us focus on our ministry.

Our new ministry was an eye-opener for the both of us. We decided to give it our one hundred percent attention. We did our first chapel service on Sunday. The chapel was small, and we could only accommodate around twelve to fifteen inmates.

Some of them looked like young boys. Katie would often say she wanted to take them home. We decided in counselling to not ask what they were in for. We decided that to win their confidence in us as chaplains, we would let them decide when they were ready to tell us.

I remember, in one service, a young man stood up to give his testimony and told us that he had killed his girlfriend because he didn't trust her. He accused her of cheating on him. I could see the look on Katie's face and knew then that taking them home was not an option. Another inmate told us in a chapel service that his girlfriend went out on the town while he had to look after her two children. Being on drugs, he drowned them in the bathtub then put them in bed as if they were sleeping.

Many of the inmates were awaiting trial. When they were sentenced, if they were given a sentence of over two years, they were transferred to a federal prison. The most difficult inmate we met was a man in his late forties awaiting trial. They released him on the weekend by mistake.

He wanted to go with us to The Salvation Army church. After church, he came home with us for lunch. When the prison authorities realized their error, they picked him up and incarcerated him again. By Monday morning, he was back in prison, and we wondered why. What a shock we got when we found out that he was a child molester. He had sexually assaulted his own daughters, and one had a child with him. He also sexually abused his grandchildren. He was sentenced to eleven years in federal prison on a Governor General's warrant, which meant he would never get out of prison unless the Governor General signed his release. That had never happened before.

I was not happy with him and told him point blank that I didn't appreciate him coming to our home for lunch with our three girls sitting at the same table. At that point, we were more cautious in counselling inmates. There are a lot of other stories I could tell.

In our second year of prison ministry, we had a visit with Chuck Colson, who was head of Prison Fellowship in the USA. He wanted to start a prison ministry in Canada. He invited all the Protestant chaplains to a barbecue on a ranch outside of Edmonton.

He wanted access to our institutions, however he didn't want to work through our chaplains. He already had two inmates who were released from the Remand Centre supporting him. We told him he had to come through the chaplaincy department at our institutions in order to start a ministry to the inmates.

When I went to the prison the following Monday, the first two inmates I saw in the holding area were the two that he had at the barbecue. I spoke to them and I knew they were embarrassed. They told me they had been arrested and taken back to the Centre, but it was a mistake. I knew then that you must be careful when dealing with inmates as they can mislead you.

That first year, I started a course with the Federal Correctional Service under the direction of the area supervisor. It was a training program in Parole Supervision and Community Assessments, with the focus on parole and assessments of inmates before being released from a federal prison.

We had some great experiences at Salvation Army events during our careers.

The second year in Edmonton, I continued my education and enrolled into a Canadian Association of Pastoral Education (CAPE) course that was offered through the University of Alberta. This course was given at the Royal Alexandra Hospital in Edmonton. It was known as the Clinical Pastoral Education Unit.

I was assigned as the chaplain to the terminally ill unit. The course was supervised by Bill Smyth, who was head of chaplaincy at the hospital.

The course ran for nine months, with five students. It was very intensive and enhanced my skill in counselling There were four units to complete before I became a CAPE Supervisor.

Katie filled in for me at the Remand Centre while I was away. She started to continue her education through home study from Athabasca University. She completed five or six courses and gained ten credits towards a university degree.

One day a young inmate who was originally from Newfoundland asked Katie if she was happily married. He said if you are not let me know and I can fix it for you. He had been charged with robbing a bank with a handgun. We thought it was funny, however it can be a part of the reality of working in a prison.

We enjoyed our two years of ministry at the Remand Centre in Edmonton. We had a beautiful group of volunteers from different churches, who were committed to the prison ministry. One couple were originally from Russia, another from Ukraine, and a couple from Africa. We knew they supported our ministry and could depend on them weekly.

Chapter 9 – Chaplains in Kingston, even to Clifford Olson

At the end of our second year, we were appointed to The Salvation Army Correctional Service in Kingston, Ontario, assisting Major Fred Mills. It was our first time ministering in the federal prison system. In Kingston and surrounding area, there were eight federal prisons. This was a new challenge for us both, with no similarities to working in a provincial prison. We did chapel services at least once a week, at all the institutions. Some months, we did a total of thirty-one services.

Each institution has its own personality and security level. Mill Haven was classed as maximum security. Collins Bay, Joyceville, Bath, Frontenac, and Pittsburgh were classed as medium security.

Kingston Penitentiary was a maximum-security facility. It had two units in the same compound and a psychiatric unit whose prisoners had no access to the general population. Across the street, the women's prison was also classed as maximum security. That prison was more difficult to work in than the other prisons. It seemed like the women inmates didn't trust anyone and always played the role of being tough to deal with.

We also visited a provincial prison in Napanee, that was our responsibility from our office in Kingston.

I went to Mill Haven weekly for chapel service for the inmates. It was difficult at times to get into the institution due to its security level. One evening, Major Mills and I were leading a service when a fight broke out between a few inmates. Fred and I managed to get them to stop and encouraged them to settle their differences on their units. They agreed, and we did our service without another incident. We knew if the guards were called in, the chapel would be shut down for a month or more.

When we were on the way out, I said to Fred, "We will read about this in the news tomorrow." Fred just smiled.

The next day, sure enough, the headlines read, "Inmate stabbed in Mill Haven Prison, one was fatally wounded." It was so different than the provincial system. I went to Mill Haven to do counselling with the inmates that requested our service. One week, I had a request from a young man who was around nineteen years old. He was having trouble with certain inmates since they wanted him for their sexual pleasures. He refused and the pressure mounted for him each day. They threatened his life and demanded that he would come to their cells at night. He was terrified. He looked like a kid, doing adult time.

I tried to get him a transfer to another institution, however that would take time. I did my best to assist him with a transfer, but the process was slow. The following week, I went to see him, but am sad to say they found him stabbed to death in his cell. This also shook me up to the realities of the federal prison system.

I visited inmates at Kingston Penitentiary on a regular basis. We also had a volunteer who came with me. John Walton was an elderly man, who was a soldier of the Kingston Citadel Corps. John was well respected in the institutions by staff and inmates. One day, he said to me, "Captain, I would like for you to visit Clifford Olson, who is in the special handling unit." He said none of the chaplains in the institution would see him, but we should be there for all inmates, regardless of their crimes. I agreed to visit him the next week when we went to the Kingston Penitentiary.

Olson was in a special unit segregated from all the other inmates. He would be escorted to the small yard close to his unit for one hour a day for exercise. He was locked in his cell for twenty-three hours every day.

When I went to this unit, there were always two guards outside the main gate. They would unlock the gate and let me in, then lock the door behind me.

The formidable and fortified Kingston Penitentiary closed in 2013.

There were cells on one side of the walkway, with each inmate locked in. Also in that unit were three inmates referred to as The Shoeshine Boy Killers: Robert Kribs, Saul Betesh, and Joe Woods. They were serving a life sentence for murdering Emannuel Jacques, a twelve-year-old boy, in downtown Toronto. I briefly spoke to them when I went to see Clifford Olson.

I started visiting this unit weekly and mostly spent time with him. He showed me documents that the government had produced to reveal children he had murdered. The federal Liberal government had paid him more than $100,000 so he would reveal where eleven children were buried after he had killed them.

The money went to Olson's wife and son. He showed me a picture of his son, who looked around four or five years old. He had blond curly hair. Olson kept this photo on the wall of his cell.

It was very difficult for me to spend time

with him, as I had three young daughters that I loved and cherished. He showed me copies of letters he wrote to different governors across the USA, advising them that there were missing children buried in certain states. I read some of the responses he received from the governors, confirming that children who were missing were never found.

Olson was a very clever inmate. Everything was always about him. The Liberal government in Ottawa was embarrassed when the news came out that they had paid him thousands of dollars. After that payout, they refused to deal with him anymore. He told me that Doug Slack, a prominent lawyer in Kingston, had signed an affidavit for him regarding the disclosure of more children buried across Canada. He also spoke with the Police Chief in Kingston.

Each interview was very intense. He wanted the police chief to see him about the other children missing. The chief refused, so Clifford told me to call them to confirm that he wanted to see them regarding this issue. I called Mr. Slack and he confirmed to me that he did sign an affidavit for Olson but said he didn't know what was in the affidavit. This document was signed on June 10th, 1983. I knew there was more to this than what he told me. No lawyer signed a document without reading it first.

I called the Police Chief in Kingston regarding my conversation with Olson, with no response. The convicted killer told me he had talked with Sergeant Peter Martin and Harry Hickling from the Kingston Police department. He was frustrated because he did not get a response from them.

One day, he gave me the name of a young girl, Karen Cook who, he thought, might be in New Brunswick. He told me her parents were Douglas and Joan Cook who lived in Moncton, New Brunswick. He said they might be living in Toronto at that point. He told me Karen was reported missing on November 28, 1957. If the Police Chief in Kingston didn't see him, he would disclose to me where Karen was buried. I was not comfortable where our conversations were going. I called Sergeant Martin at the police station and told him what Olson was up to. I was upset and didn't want to be involved with Olson any longer.

I didn't want to hear where this child was buried and told the police that they needed to see Olson and clear up this issue. I was exhausted physically, spiritually, and mentally from my encounter with Olson.

I wanted to stop seeing him. Sergeant. Martin understood my predicament and assured me he would visit Olson and deal with this issue. I have handwritten notes on file regarding the issues that Olson raised, signed by him. That was the last time I saw Clifford Olson.

INSTITUTIONAL INTERVIEW

Inst. _J.P._ Date _Jan. 5/84_
NAME _Clifford Olson_ d.o.b. _____
Inst. No. _____ Cell Location _____
C.O. _____ Work Area _____

REQUEST: Karen Cook
Nov. 28/1957 (parents Toronto)
(Douglas & Joan Cook)

ACTION TAKEN: Moncton N.B.
(Harry Hickling Jan 1977 last seen
Sgt. Pt. Martin)
Aug 18/83 affid 10 June 1983
Doug Slack - Lawyer

FURTHER ACTION REQUIRED:
549-4660
Albert Murphy

Transferred to _____ on date of _____
Called Sgt Martin
Jan 19/84 advising the above
gave me for support to work with
about it and is willing information is
me & disclosed respecting the above

INSTITUTIONAL INTERVIEW

Captain King.

Inst. ___KP___ Date __Jan 12, 84__
NAME __Wm. Clifford__ d.o.b. _____
Inst. No. _____ Cell Location _____
C.O. _____ Work Area _____

REQUEST: Have you had a chance to work out the Parents in regards to KAREN COOK. I also mentioned that I talked to Sgt Peter Morten + Harry HICKLING of the Kingston POLICE on THIS

ACTION TAKEN: Clifford. I ask John to give you this message.

We also conducted chapel services within Kingston Penitentiary. At times, we had more than forty inmates in the chapel for each service. It gave them an opportunity to leave their units and share fellowship with others in the institution.

One evening, we were conducting a chapel service with Major Fred Mills, his wife Major Doreen Mills, and volunteer John Walton. Major Fred was leading the service and I was playing my piano accordion for the singing.

It was normal for inmates to ask one of us to see them outside the chapel door in the hallway. I saw Major Doreen leave the chapel with an inmate. It was a while before she returned. She came up to afterward and said to me, "Don't let that inmate get close to me." When the service was over, the inmates started to walk down the hallway to their units. I walked behind Doreen and blocked this inmate from coming near her.

After we cleared security and left the institution, Doreen told us what happened. That inmate had tried to sexually assault her. She fended him off until she was able to get back into the chapel with us. Fred reported it to the administration as Kingston Penitentiary and they investigated this issue.

What they found out shocked us all. That inmate was had been transferred from a psychiatric ward in Northern Ontario. His papers stated that he was to be in solitary confinement as he was classed as a dangerous offender. He arrived the same day we were scheduled for chapel service, and the guards had not checked his paperwork before they let him come to chapel.

This was an experience that shook us all. If he had harmed Doreen, the other inmates would have done him in right in the hallway before they went back to their units.

I also visited Joyceville Institution and did counselling and chapel services for its inmates. This institution was totally different than the maximum-security institutions. There were several inmates from Newfoundland serving three- to five-year sentences; one was doing a life sentence for murdering his aunt. I took him out on day parole for his first outing since he was incarcerated and discovered he was originally from the Catalina area. When his wife and son

Katie and I worked together and had a great life together.

came to Kingston to visit him, she and her son stayed at our house. This inmate was what we called an albino person. Katie didn't trust him and we were both cautious around him. However, our commitment was to ministry, and we never excluded anyone or refused their requests for companionship.

Katie started a course through the Canadian Association of Pastoral Education and was supervised by the head chaplain in the Kingston Penitentiary, Don Misner. Katie would visit this institution weekly with the four other chaplains on this course. I continued working at the other institutions in Kingston and assisting inmates with their release plans. A number of them applied to attend our addiction programs at Salvation Army centres across Ontario that were required after their releases.

Katie was very skilled in counselling people one on one. People would confide in her with their personal problems and trust her judgement when she gave them advise.

She worked with clients at the family court in Kingston and Judge Ken Pedlar would assign clients to her as needed. Katie enjoyed her work under Judge Pedlar and helped a lot of clients who were going through a difficult time.

Chapter 10 – A Fresh Start in Our Work and Family

During our first year in Kingston, Katie and I were going through personal difficulties in our relationship. The prison ministry contributed to this strain. I came to a point that I refused to stay in Corrections in Kingston and wanted a transfer. However, Katie did not support this idea.

When we finished our first year, we transferred to the Family Service Department in Kingston. It was under the direction of the Kingston Citadel Corps. We moved from our residence on Mack Street to the old quarters on Frontenac Street. This was an old house that needed lots of repairs and upkeep.

We were still struggling with our relationship, and things didn't improve much while we were in Kingston. I knew every relationship has its own issues somewhere in life, which need to be dealt with and discussed by both with an open mind.

The second year, while in Family Services, I enrolled in a unit of the Canadian Association of Pastoral Education at Queens University. That unit was referred to as a Supervised Pastoral Education Unit. I attended Queens University weekly for nine months. Our supervisors were professors Oakley Dwyer and Doug Perry. This was my second unit through the Canadian Association of Pastoral Education.

After two years there, we were transferred to Sudbury, Ontario as the corps officers. It was a welcome move for me, and I looked forward to this new appointment. We were the first Newfoundlanders appointed as corps officers to the Sudbury Corps.

Half of the congregation were from Newfoundland, working in the mines. The other half were from Sudbury and the surrounding area.

Our family portrait with our daughters and Katie's parents Walter and Elsie.

Our first year went great. We enjoyed our ministry to the fullest. Our congregation consisted of around fifty to sixty people per service. We also had a Family Service department. Ruth

Lambert supervised that department. We had a good working relationship with her.

We could have stayed longer than three years; however, due to difficulties with the Public relations officer, we left earlier than expected. We had questioned a fundraising event in the shopping mall as we considered it a gambling ploy. The people in the corps supported my concern, and I reported it to my Divisional Commander. He took side with the public relations officer, without coming to Sudbury and investigating it himself. Finally, they stopped this event as it was against the Salvation Army's policy regarding gambling.

Regardless, the Divisional Commander made what I call an unfair decision and moved us out of Sudbury instead of moving the public relations officer. It was that employee's first year in Sudbury, and we had been there for three years, so the Divisional Commander transferred us out.

It was sad because we had to leave Yvette

behind in Sudbury, as she was enrolled in the nursing program, while Michelle was enrolled in Georgian College in Barrie in the interior designing program. We were very upset, to say the least, when we had to leave them behind due to a poor decision by our Divisional Commander.

Next, we went to Brandon Citadel, in Manitoba. It was disappointing for us to leave Sudbury, however, once again, we were committed to ministry with the Salvation Army, so we packed up and moved: Katie, Rochelle and I, along with her friend, Shannon Hurley, who was our neighbour in Kingston.

We arrived in Brandon on Sunday evening and went directly to our residence. There was a message on the phone for us to come right away to the airport, as they were evacuating Indigenous people from God's Lake Narrows and the surrounding area due to forest fires that threatened their communities.

The Salvation Army was responsible for providing snacks, sandwiches, etc. at the airport to the people during this evacuation. We were also responsible for recruiting volunteers to assist them after they were placed in the different hotels and gyms in the city. The military evacuated them with their Hercules aircraft, while we worked in cooperation with the Social Services in Brandon. We and our volunteers were at the airport twenty-four hours each day for two weeks before we got settled into our new home.

We were a part of the Emergency Measures Operation (EMO) and had a special permit to park our vehicles anywhere to get supplies for the evacuated adults and children. There were more than 1,600 men, women, and children flown in. We had all the hotels, motels, gyms etc. booked to accommodate them.

We would order dozens of donuts and large supplies of cookies, coffee, and milk at Tim Horton's for the adults and children until they were placed in a suitable location to stay until this crisis was over. They would put it on a tab for the EMO. It was busy and exhausting for us all. Some days Katie and I did not sleep. It was quite an initiation on our first visit to Brandon.

Late in the morning on July 26th, Katie came upstairs at the airport and wished me happy anniversary. We both almost forgot due to being so busy.

After all the people that Brandon could accommodate were evacuated, they focused on Winnipeg and continued transporting people out of the danger zone where the fires were spreading. We then moved from the airport to an office downtown where we continued to recruit volunteers to assist the people who were displaced. We had more than three hundred volunteers on a list that we called when needed at the different sites.

The social services department also issued cheques to families and individuals who needed assistance. This created a problem, especially at the hotels and motels. The evacuees purchased alcohol, beer, and wine, then got drunk and caused a lot of problems. There was a lot of damage done to the hotel rooms as toilets overflowed, etc. They created a mess. Keep in mind that a lot of these people had never been off their reservation before and were not familiar with life in a hotel room.

After the forest fires were under control, the military set up at the airport to fly the evacuees back to their community. We had a thrift store in Brandon and donated two garbage bags of clothing for each family that needed it. When they went to the airport, the military refused to transport all these bags of clothing back to the reservation. The evacuees sat down on the tarmac and refused to go without their bags of clothing.

After much deliberating with their superiors and government officials, the military decided to transport these items with the people to their destination. This took several days until everyone returned home.

Now, we had to try and settle into our own

responsibility at the corps. First, we needed several days to rest and get ourselves sorted out and debriefed due to the stress we had gone through. The people of Brandon were very kind to us during this transition; they supported us in the community and in our ministry at the corps.

In our second year there, I received a call from a friend in Kingston, informing me that Laura, my son Mike's mother, wanted me to call her. I was curious as to what she wanted. Katie was also nervous about this as it had been years with no contact from them.

    I decided to return her call. Laura informed me that Mike wanted to talk to me as he and his partner had a child and he wanted to know my medical history. I called him from my office, and he indicated they were coming to Edmonton from Fort McMurray. We decided to meet them in Edmonton. Katie was upset not knowing what this was all about.

We checked into a hotel and waited for them to come by. Mike and his wife Deanne had a beautiful little daughter, named Ashleigh, who won our hearts when we first met her. We had a good visit and went over a lot of things and tried to fill in the gaps. At that time, Mike was only concerned about medical issues.

Although we didn't meet until Mike was an adult, we became close friends.

We spent the day together at the Edmonton Mall and really enjoyed our time together. Katie and I told them that they could come see us anytime.

We then went back to Brandon and got involved in our ministry. Brandon's Corps had a small congregation and had financial difficulties to meet the needs of their pastors and the church.

One day I received a call from the Fatheringham family, whose parents had a special relationship with The Salvation Army. Mr. Fatheringham had a donation for me to pick up as he didn't want to put it in the mail.

I went to his office and he told me his parents had requested that the interest from their estate was to go to The Salvation Army. He gave me a cheque for three hundred and twenty thousand dollars, and another one hundred and eighty thousand would come when the estate was finished. His parents wanted the Brandon Corps to have five hundred thousand and five hundred thousand for the Salvation Army in Winnipeg.

I notified the Divisional Commander and he advised me it had to go to the public relations department in Toronto. The Fotheringham family specifically wanted it to be used in Brandon, however I was informed by the Army that it had to go to Territorial Headquarter (THQ).

I was transferred a year later to Ontario and never saw any of these funds used in the Brandon Corps, where it was needed.

I received news that the Federal Correctional Services had a new manager coming to the city as the head of their department. Having experience in Correctional Services, with community assessments and Parole Supervision I made an appointment to see him when he got settled in his office. I had a good visit with him and discovered he needed assistance with supervision and assessments. He gave me a contract to provide these services when needed. This worked great for me as I never did like having socials to finance the church.

I did several assessments and parole supervisions each month and received a cheque for more than $800 monthly. This was good for the corps and I didn't have to bother with fundraising events.

These contracts had to be signed by the Army's correctional department at THQ in Toronto. Major Bram Meekings was responsible for these contracts. During his visit out west conducting inspections at the correctional services department in each province, he asked if he could drop in to see Katie and I in Brandon. We were pleased to see him as we had worked under his direction before. He was impressed that we had a contract with the government to provide services, even though we weren't involved with his department. He wanted to know if we were interested in coming back to his department again. If we were, we could write him a letter confirming our interest.

We told him we would not write such a letter, however if he wanted us back in corrections, we were willing to take an appointment if given the opportunity. We never gave it any more thought. We just went ahead with our ministry.

The following March, we had a call from our Divisional Commander Major Baden Marshall, informing us that THQ was interested in giving us an appointment in the Correctional Service Department. He indicated he was sorry to see us leave. However, if we were receptive to it, he would support our decision. We really appreciated the support that he gave us during our two years in Brandon.

Courageous Army fire fighters receive awards

WINNIPEG, Man. — Major and Mrs. John Phelan of Portage la Prairie and Captain and Mrs. Edgar King of Brandon were given appreciation awards by the government of Manitoba following a dinner at the Manitoba Legislative Building. The awards were for "exemplary service during the evacuation of northern residents during the forest fires which burned much of northern Manitoba during July and August 1989."

Shown are (l. to r.) The Honourable Albert Driedger, Minister of Government Services, Province of Manitoba; Major and Mrs. Phelan; Mrs. Captain Katie King; Captain King; Mr. F. Zeggil, Manitoba Emergency Measures Organization

We were invited to a luncheon in Winnipeg to honour the Salvation Army for the role they played in the evacuation. We were presented with a plaque with our names engraved on it, and the government officials expressed their thanks for the work we did.

Not only did we counsel married couples that year, our eldest daughter Yvette also got married during our third year in Peterborough.

Chapter 11 – The Peterborough Years

In May, we received a letter from THQ with our new appointment. I was appointed as the Executive Director of the Correctional Department in Peterborough and Katie was appointed as the Director of Operations. We had a staff of six people, with several contracts with the federal and provincial governments.

We were excited to move back to Ontario as it was closer for Katie to visit her parents in Newfoundland. They often came and stayed with us for the winter.

Mike, Deanne and Ashleigh came to Peterborough for a visit. This gave Michelle and Yvette an opportunity to meet him and his family. Yvette, being the oldest girl, was very close to me and wasn't sure about Mike at first. She told Katie if Mike looked like me, she would accept him as her brother.

We went to Niagara Falls together. Mike and I were walking ahead of everyone, chatting, and Yvette was watching us. Katie told me afterward that when she saw us walking together, Yvette said to her, "My God, Mom. Look at them. They look so much alike." That confirmed to her that Mike was her brother. We laughed later when she told me.

In our third year in Peterborough, Katie and I decided to continue with our education in a new field of study. We enrolled in the American Accreditation of Marriage Enrichment (ACME). We wanted to enhance our skill in marriage counselling. To get certified, we had to take a special program in St. Paul's University, Minnesota.

We drove down to Minnesota and did an intensive program to get our qualifications. We finally got our certificate and were qualified to counsel couples who had a good relationship. We augmented our studies with two seminars in Nova Scotia and one in Newfoundland. We also did several pre-marital counselling sessions for different religious groups.

In Peterborough, we had a provincial halfway house, which received inmates from the jail before they were released back into the community. We also had a contract with the provincial government for our shoplifter program. People who were caught shoplifting were sent to our diversion program before they went before a judge. If they completed our program, their charges would be dropped, and they would not get a record for that offence. This contract was for more than $40,000 yearly.

We also had a parole supervision and community assessment contract with the Federal Correctional Department to provide services for inmates released from the Warkworth

Institution. This contract was worth $90,000 to $100,000 annually. We were also responsible for visiting the Warkworth Institution to assist inmates who were being released back into the communities across Ontario. We would process their applications for placement at our addictions centres, as required by the government prior to release.

Additionally, we were responsible for assisting inmates in Millbrook Provincial Prison, who were waiting for release, and wanted to take our addiction-recovery programs offered across Ontario.

Katie and I were busy at different institutions, counselling inmates, helping with pre-release plans, and conducting chapel services weekly. Katie had a part-time chaplain working under her direction in the provincial centres. Meanwhile, I visited the federal prison in Warkworth, with my parole supervisor, assisting inmates with the issues they were interested in addressing.

We had a shoplifting counsellor, working in our office. Muriel Stellar was great at counselling men and women who were enrolled in our program. She worked with judges in Lindsay and Peterborough who released clients to our program. Muriel was well respected by the judges and lawyers at the different courts.

Jim Rose was the director at our provincial halfway house where we had around eight to ten clients on a regular basis.

What I didn't know when I came into this appointment was that the previous officer in charge had a problem with the federal area manager of the correctional department in Peterborough. Ian Harmston led the department and the officer before me had no experience in Correctional Services. He didn't understand the protocol for dealing with his office. Before I came to Peterborough, Ian decided to not renew the contract with The Salvation Army because of the incompetence of the former officer.

I made an appointment to see him at his

office, so we set a date and time to meet. He explained why he had cancelled our contract. Apparently, the former

executive officer had limited experience and didn't understand what his responsibility entailed.

I shared with him my experience with correctional services and how I was familiar with the contracting process, having had contracts with the federal government before I came to Peterborough.

He said point blank, "I appreciate your experience and knowledge of our department. I don't blame you or your office in Peterborough for what happened."

"However," he said, "I am disappointed with The Salvation Army, who should have known better. I can't believe the Army would appoint that asshole to run their correctional service department in Peterborough."

He didn't mince words as he expressed how he felt towards the Army. I appreciated his frankness and understood where he was coming from.

When the contract ended, I had to let the parole supervisor go. We hired him at the provincial halfway house, under the direction of Mr. Rose. Due to the lost revenue from that contract, I had to lay off our part-time chaplain, who was not happy with that decision. The extra funds we received paid for these other programs.

I met with the Provincial Correctional Services area manager, and he too was concerned with the way the previous officer had conducted himself. He told me, in no uncertain terms, that he was also disappointed with that officer, who was very unprofessional in his dealings with his department. He was thinking about cancelling the shoplifting program.

After my visit with him, and my assurances that it would be different with me being responsible for our services, he decided to keep that contract going. It continued for the five years until I moved to another appointment.

It was a challenge keeping everything in balance during my first year in Peterborough. Things seemed to be moving forward slowly until we got settled in. The shoplifting program was highly successful, and we had around twelve to fourteen clients on a regular basis.

We did a lot of pre-release planning with inmates in Millbrook Correctional Centre and Warkworth Institution, referring them to our addiction-treatment centres across Ontario.

Rochelle completed her Grade 12 education and enrolled at the College for the Social Work Program. She and Bill Bowers went to their graduation together in a limousine they rented for this special event. A week before, Bill had shaved his head, not thinking about the graduation party and photos. I don't think Rochelle was impressed.

Everything was going great for the first two to three years, then a series of serious issues came up. Katie was working in the Millbrook

Correctional Centre regarding placements that were approved by the program director and the head of the social services for inmates. As part of her role, she planned for an inmate, Clint Cusack, to be placed in our treatment centre in Hamilton in September 1993. Her colleagues classed him as a model prisoner and supported his release. She thought that they had disclosed all the issues that were important regarding his placement.

They released him and before the end of the month, he took off without permission. He went to Sudbury and met up with another guy who had a record for drug charges. A young police officer in Sudbury pulled their car over because it had a broken taillight. When Constable Joe McDonald was approaching their car, Cusack got out and shot him twice in the chest. The officer died on the street by his car. Cusack and his accomplice had a large quantity of drugs in the car and thought he stopped them for that. This shook us all up, as our son-in-law

Tim is with the RCMP and was friends with McDonald.

They finally caught Cusack, arrested him for murder, and started an investigation into his release. Katie was called and had to attend a hearing in Hamilton. At first, it appeared they were trying to blame her and The Salvation Army for sending him to their treatment centre. Katie had assumed that they had given her all the information for his application before he was accepted into the program, and they approved his release.

After a week or two, the truth started to come out. The program director and head of the social service department in Millbrook, had not disclosed all the concerns on Cusack's file. It appeared that they were trying to avoid their responsibility for this inmate's release and pass the blame onto The Salvation Army.

When the investigation was over, the results confirmed the management at Millbrook were responsible for his release. As we discovered later, Cusack had a lot of problems during his incarceration in Millbrook Correctional Centre, which were not disclosed to the Army before the decision to accept him in their program.

The Army was absolved of any responsibility for this inmate's release. This was a relief to us all, especially Katie, who was put through this ordeal. We were happy that finally it was over, and we could go back to work at our designated institutions.

That didn't last long; we ran into another issue with the director at the Peterborough Jail. Gary Pickering and his wife Eva were our next-door neighbours. Gary was the superintendent at the jail, and we had a contract through his department for our provincial halfway house. Its director, Jim Rose, was interviewing for a new staff position at our centre. Eva applied for the job but didn't have any experience working with inmates.

Jim brought it to our attention, and we

made it clear to him it was his responsibility to hire someone with the right experience. Being neighbours and friends, Eva assumed she would get this job. We indicated to her that we weren't involved in the hiring process.

Jim hired a man who had a lot of experience working with inmates, federally and provincially. When Gary and Eva found out, they went ballistic. They not only blamed Jim, but also blamed us for not hiring Eva. It was a very difficult time for us all to say the least. They threatened to sue The Salvation Army and started to use the race card. Eva was originally from Poland so they tried to use that to imply discrimination. They were going to report us to the government and make a case out of it.

We had to go to THQ, who were responsible for our work in Peterborough. We met with Major David Moulton, our department head, and informed him of this situation.

David was trying to be nice in dealing with the Pickerings but they didn't respond to him. They threatened the Army. Gary was going to report us to the provincial government but wasn't going to say that his wife was the one who was filing a complaint against the Army.

In our last meeting with Major Moulton, I suggested that he write a letter to Gary that stated that it was his wife, Eva who was making a complaint over our hiring practices, and let Gary know he was sending a copy to the government officials in charge of his department. Then he would wait for a response from him before contacting the government. I said that this should solve the issue, as Gary would be in a conflict of interest and the government would take issue with that.

David agreed to do so and sent Gary a letter. We thought the issue was resolved; however, this was not so. Gary gave up on that issue but created another one. He asked the government for a transfer and indicated to them that they weren't getting value for their money at the Kawartha halfway house. He suggested that they didn't need placements for the inmates as the jail was going to close in the years ahead, because a new jail was under construction in Lindsay.

The government had just spent $450,000 on repairs and re-modelling the house. They came back and decided not to renew the contract with The Salvation Army and transferred Gary to a different position in Ottawa. I guess he ultimately got his revenge for Eva not getting the position at our halfway house.

The last year I was in Peterborough, we closed the halfway house. Here we had an empty building, totally renovated, with no clients.

A new area manager took over the Federal Correctional Services in Peterborough, as Ian Hermanson had retired. I made an appointment to see him, and we went over the past relationship with his former colleague. I knew he was having trouble placing federal inmates in small centres in Peterborough. I told him about the Kawartha house and all the renovations. We did a tour and he was impressed by it and wanted it for a federal halfway house. The building was empty, but not officially closed, so we decided to pursue this issue.

Because it was closed as a provincial halfway house, we would have to get approval from the city to license it as a federal facility.

We set up a meeting with Mayor Jack Doris and laid out our plans for this building. However, the mayor was not really on board. He was open to our suggestion; however, he was not ready to support our plans.

We discussed it further and the area manager suggested that we get a contract signed for the building by the Federal Correctional Services. He came up with a contract for $100,000, so that we could keep it open, pay all our expenses and taxes, and hire a couple of employees to be at the house day and night. Every month, we received a cheque from the federal government for $10,000 to maintain the building and pay employees as security for it.

In March, The Salvation Army Correctional Department in Toronto was going through restructuring and they decided to put our department in Peterborough under the Divisional Commander. Major Bob Moulton was in this role during this transition. I met with him to see what plans he had for our department. He told me the Correctional Services in Peterborough would come under the supervision of the Peterborough Corps and indicated it would be supervised locally. I knew I was then on the list to move in June.

I informed the Federal Correctional Area manager and gave him the news. He wanted to contact the Divisional Commander regarding our plans and ask for me to stay in Peterborough until the project came online.

I told him if he called the Divisional Commander, he would think that I put him up to it. He decided to call anyway and was told by the DC that the officer coming in to replace me had experience in Correctional Work, and things would be fine.

We were transferred to the Salvation Army Correctional Services in Halifax with me as the Executive Director and Katie as the Director of Programs. We moved to Halifax the end of June.

The officer who came to Peterborough was on sick leave when he started this appointment and less than three months later, his wife had a breakdown. They were home until they moved them out at the end of June the following year. I am sure the area manager was disappointed in the Army for the poor decision they made to replace us.

Chapter 12 – Navigating Rough Seas in Halifax

We were happy to be appointed to Halifax as we were closer to Newfoundland so Katie could visit her parents, who had a lot of health concerns.

Before we left Peterborough, I talked to the DC in Halifax, Major Bill Radcliffe. He informed me that our residence would be in an apartment in Halifax and that was all they were providing for us. I talked to the single, female officer we were replacing, and she told me the apartment was for one person. I called THQ in Toronto and spoke to Commissioner Don Kerr, the Territorial Commander and explained the situation.

He told me they would have to have a house to accommodate us before we arrived in Halifax. He would advise them that was what he required. The next day I had a call from the DC, telling me that they would have a house for us. He wanted to know when we were taking our vacation so they could get on it right away.

I told him we were going on vacation for five weeks before we came to our new appointment. This would give them time to find and purchase a house for us. He apologized for our earlier conversation and assured me that I had his support. We appreciated it as we knew him well and respected him as our Divisional Commander.

When we left Peterborough, Rochelle was in her second year at Sir Sandford Fleming College in Peterborough. She had enrolled in the Early Childhood Education Program. We left her behind when we moved. We vacationed in Newfoundland for five weeks then headed to Halifax.

The day before we arrived, I had a call from the program director, Major Harold Robins. They had a new residence awaiting us on

Charlois Court in Dartmouth and it would be furnished and set up before we arrived the next day. We would live in Dartmouth and work in downtown Halifax. We had to cross the toll bridge twice a day when we went back and forth. This would be an inconvenience every day.

We were also responsible for a federal halfway house in Dartmouth and a halfway house in Sydney for young offenders. The youth facility had a contract with the provincial government for $500,000 annually. This was enough funds to operate the centre and pay our staff a decent salary. The maximum number of youths we could accommodate was five. This centre was managed by Director Heather Paruch, who was very competent and professional with the clients and her staff. We gave this centre minimal oversight, as the staff were well qualified.

Katie and I usually visited it once a month, and attended divisional meetings held for the officers in the area. All the programs were under the direction of the Divisional Commander.

We also had a Women's Institute in Windsor area, that my staff attended on a regular basis. Our staff consisted of an office manager, Nancy Young, a chaplain, Major Rowena Wiseman, a parole supervisor, and a court worker named Betty Peyton.

The parole supervision contract was coming to an end and the federal government did not renew it before we moved at the end of our second year.

Meanwhile, Railton House, the federal halfway house in Dartmouth, was operating on a shoestring budget. The contract did not fund it adequately for the needs of this centre. There were no funds for maintenance or to keep the property updated as needed. The contract with the federal government gave us what they felt was needed, and that was way short of the finances we actually needed to operate this centre.

Our contract ended on March 30th each year.

I was told by my Divisional Commander to negotiate a contract with the government that would cover all costs for operations. If they did not provide the funds needed, The Salvation Army would not sign a contract as they had before. I drew up a budget and presented it to the area manager, with all the items we needed to be funded to operate our centre. I got the impression that he was not receptive to negotiating with me, since I was experienced with the federal government process.

He had a representative from the head office in Moncton come to Halifax and go over the details before a contract was approved. We met, and I went over each line in my budget and explained what the extra funds were for. We needed them for maintenance on the building that was direly needed. The inside of the centre needed renovations to the bathrooms and windows need to be replaced.

The total budget I requested was more than

$300,000. He agreed with me totally, supported the budget I had prepared and confirmed that it was a reasonable amount for operating our centre.

Also, our staff hadn't received a raise in salary for more than six years. The staff consisted of a director, a business manager, a cook, and three to four staff on shift twenty-four hours a day.

I knew the area manager would take issue with the budget, as he had total control before I came in as the new executive director for all correctional operations for the Salvation Army in Nova Scotia.

The last week of February 1997, I issued layoff notices to all our employees at Railton House, giving them thirty days' notice in case the government did not sign a new contract. The director and staff were not pleased with this decision, but I was only doing what my Divisional Commander required. At times, the director would not cooperate with the decisions that we made and blamed it on me.

I told her time and time again that I was following orders that were given to be by the Divisional Commander. I got to a point where I had the Divisional Commander and the program director meet in his office to explain our situation. She was reluctant to attend but had to at the request of the divisional leaders. In that meeting, they laid out the reality of our situation and told her if she didn't cooperate with me, she would be dismissed from her duties at our centre.

At times it was very tense in our discussions regarding the new contract we wanted. After that meeting, she settled down and informed our staff what the situation was about. They were all under stress as they didn't want to lose their jobs working at Railton House.

On March 29th, I got a call from the representative they brought in to negotiate the contract. He told me that the area manager, Ron Lawyer, would not approve our budget and we would get the same funding as per the last budget. I told him to advise the area manager that he would have to remove all his clients on March 31st when our contract ended.

He was very understanding and agreed with me that I had presented a reasonable budget. He told me I would receive the budget and a contract for the Army to sign by the next day.

The pressure was on. All my staff were nervous, especially the director and Railton House staff.

I knew the area manager was bluffing, as they had no other placement option for their federal clients that were being released from prison.

The next day, I waited in my office for a response. A courier delivered a large brown envelope and gave it to my business manager. She came into my office and handed me the envelope. Everyone was nervous. When I opened it and looked at the documents, the contract was for the full amount I asked for in my budget.

I had called his bluff and won.

The director and staff were delighted. They received a raise in pay, the first one in seven years. Now I was praised for the work I did, but before they hardly spoke to me. I understood that and continued to support and work with them.

Chapter 13 – Fighting Cancer

Just when it seemed like everything was going great, Katie and I were faced with another issue. This one was personal. She had felt a lump in her breast the week before we left Peterborough.

Our doctor told her to see about it when we got settled in Halifax. She went to a doctor, and he sent her to the hospital to get a biopsy done. We were in Sydney, attending a divisional meeting when she received a call from our secretary, directing Katie to phone the doctor regarding her results. We were both shaken as we suspected something serious was happening.

The doctor informed her the lump was malignant and she needed surgery to have it removed. It shook us to the core. This was not what we had expected. Even the doctor said, "It may be just a mass of tissue." However, that was not so.

They scheduled surgery for her within a week and she was admitted to the hospital in Halifax. After removing this lump, they told her the cancer was in her lymph nodes, and we knew it was serious.

She started chemotherapy treatments that went on for a couple of months, which also affected her health. After chemo, she had to do radiation treatments. We were caught up in a nightmare. I went with her for every appointment and sat with her when she received every chemo treatment.

We were devastated with this ordeal we were facing together. We cried together, held each other, and prayed together about this disease.

After three or four chemo treatments, Katie started losing her hair. This was so difficult for her. It was sad to see her going through this.

I remember one morning she was in the shower and her hair was falling out. She was crying. I went to her and held her, and we cried together. It was so difficult for us both. We were both suffering together.

Before her hair was totally gone, she decided to get her head shaved and wear a wig when out in public. We had a friend from Ming's Bight, Donna Clarke, who now lived in Halifax. She was a hairdresser and had a shop downtown. Donna came by and shaved Katie's head, then fitted her with a wig that matched her own hair. It gave Katie confidence to go out in public again.

After all the treatments were finished, Katie went back to the specialist for a check-up. He told Katie to go on with her life since everything was good.

Two of our daughters, Michelle and Yvette, were living in British Columbia. We decided to ask for a transfer out there to be close to them during her recovery. Michelle had a son named Connor, and Yvette had a daughter, Miranda, so we looked forward in seeing them again and spending time with their families.

The Salvation Army advised us that there were no correctional appointments available in B.C. We told them we would take a corps appointment if there was one available. They appointed us as the pastors to the Salvation Army Penticton Community Church. We then started packing to move. At that time, Rochelle was living at home, and Bill was also living with us in our basement. They had made plans to stay in Halifax and get an apartment together.

We assumed Rochelle would go with us to B.C. I guess love changes everything when you are young. They decided to stay in Nova Scotia.

We went on vacation in Newfoundland before we started our journey across

Canada to our new appointment in British Columbia. We had a good vacation, visiting around the island. Katie missed her mom, who had passed away while we were living in Peterborough.

Her father had stayed with us the first winter in Halifax, since he had difficulty adjusting since Elsie passed away. The second year in Halifax, Katie wasn't well enough to have him with us for the winter. We were devastated with her having to face surgery, then chemo and radiation.

When we arrived in Penticton, it was a beautiful city, however the temperature was beyond what we expected. With no central air in our quarters, it felt like we were in a sauna. The first thing we did was to have it installed so we could live comfortably.

The Community Church concept was totally different for us both. When we went to our first service, the protocol was for us, as the pastors to sit in the front of the church. The worship team led the congregational singing for the first twenty to twenty-five minutes. When they finished, we went to the platform and led the rest of the worship service. I delivered the message, then the worship team led the singing until the service ended.

It took time for us to adjust to this new format. It was a learning experience for us both.

We settled in and really enjoyed this new style of worship; we had a great team in our church that gave us their undivided support. Our church was very new, a beautiful building that was totally paid for.

We also had a shelter funded two thirds by the provincial government and we funded the remainder. We had two thrift stores and a family service department with a food bank for the area.

Our staff included a director for the family services, and food bank operator, and a director at our shelter. At my office, we also had an accountant, two secretaries, a youth pastor, and many dedicated volunteers. We had around twenty-five staff in total on our payroll.

The first year, everything fell into place. Katie was back to her normal self after going through such a difficult ordeal with her health. However, after December, she started having pain in her hips and went to the doctor about it.

He said it was arthritis, however she sensed that this was not so.

He sent her to a massage therapist but that didn't help with the pain. They asked her if she discussed this with her doctor. Katie told them what her doctor said. We decided to go on vacation the end of June and headed down east, with the possibility of going to Newfoundland. When we stopped at a hotel in Medicine Hat, I had a call from Newfoundland telling me my brother Frank had passed away.

This was devastating for us both, as Katie and I were close to Frank. We had always enjoyed our time with him. When he had open heart surgery in St. John's three years earlier, we were there for him. Everything had been going fine since, then he had an aneurism on his brain, went into a coma, and didn't survive.

When we arrived in Ontario, we decided to visit our friends Fred and Shirley Ash in Oakville. Katie was having severe pains in her hips, so we decided to cut short our vacation and return to B.C. When we got back to Penticton, Katie made an appointment to see her doctor again. He still insisted that her problem was arthritis in her joints.

We were very concerned as Katie had had cancer and had taken all these treatments. The pain continued to increase with no let-up day and night.

At the end of September, her doctor booked an appointment in Kelowna at the cancer clinic to have a scan and further tests done. We went to Kelowna in the middle of September and waited for the results.

The specialist at the hospital in Penticton was concerned that they didn't remove Katie's breast, and only removed the lump.

He stressed that it was important to do so to prevent cancer from coming back in the same breast. Katie received a call from our friends the Goodbridge, Alice had breast cancer. Without hesitation Katie told her to have her breast removed, it probably would give her a better chance of surviving.

Alice had her surgery and is still living today after twenty-two years.

I'm sure she appreciated the advice Katie gave her.

On September 29th, we got Katie's report from the doctor. It was devastating: cancer had spread through her system. The specialist told Katie she had around six months at most to live. We were heartbroken with this news.

We were numb, angry, grieving in our hearts and spirit. Katie said, "Today, I received my death sentence." We held each other and cried in agony, feeling loss, asking why this was happening to us. Life ended for the both of us at that moment. Here we were expecting a good report and had made plans to go out for dinner. Now, our world came crashing down around us. All we wanted then was our daughters with us. We needed them and they were there to support us.

Katie said that she felt that God had left her alone that day, to suffer on her own. She recorded it all in her diary, which she wrote in daily.

The doctor gave her strong medication for the pain; however, we knew the reality that lay ahead for us both.

Yvette announced she was pregnant, before she went back home to Maple Ridge. Rochelle was coming for Christmas. She and Bill were planning to get married in B.C. after Christmas. This brought a bit of sunshine in our lives.

Dr. Ming came to our residence and apologized to Katie for treating her for arthritis and sciatica. When she saw him in his clinic, he again expressed how he felt and wept in Katie's presence.

We knew he was genuinely sorry for not treating her as a cancer patient. October 5th,

1999, was the last date Katie wrote in her diary.

She was on strong pain pills and felt high every day. She knew these pills were addictive, but they controlled the pain. On Sunday, Oct. 7th, Katie was so weak she couldn't get out of bed. I called the ambulance and they admitted her at the Penticton hospital.

That day they only had minimal staff on duty, so they kept her in the emergency unit until Monday, when they would move her on a ward. She was hooked up to an oxygen supply, and a nurse was on duty to supervise her hourly and give her pain meds when she needed them. Katie had a book, written by Chuck Swindoll, on her bed. When she fell asleep, the nurse borrowed it and went to a sitting room to read it.

Katie woke an hour later and couldn't breathe. She was too weak to get the nurse's attention. Finally, the nurse came back and they realized the oxygen tank was empty. She had neglected her duty as she was supposed to sit by Katie's bed in case she needed anything. It was two hours before they got another oxygen tank set up and hooked up to her line.

Katie was so weak from the ordeal that they had to postpone several tests they had planned to do Monday morning. I was upset and reported it to the specialist. He filed a complaint against the nurse.

They finally did blood work and a scan of Katie's heart. The doctor told us half of Katie's heart had shut down. She was so weak that they had to cancel several other tests they required. They moved her to a private room by the ICU, on October 19. She was getting weaker each day.

The doctor called me into his office on October 20th and told me Katie wouldn't make it to the weekend. I went back to her room while the doctor told Katie the sad news. Yvette arrived and Michelle and Rochelle and Bill were on the way. Their plane got delayed in Vancouver and they were late getting to Penticton.

Katie looked at me and said, "Who will look after you when I am gone?" She was more

Katie's gravesite in Trout River, Newfoundland

concerned about me than herself.

That is the kind of woman she was, always there for other people. Rochelle and Bill arrived at the hospital on Oct. 22nd, at 10 p.m. They told Katie they had their marriage license and would get married in her room the next day. Katie was so excited and so proud of her girls. They were so special to us both. Rochelle had her wedding dress and was ready to get married. Katie said she could have her rings if she wanted them. We left the hospital around 11 p.m. and went back

My brother Frank, me and Ken

Our family members met in the morning. Rochelle and Bill were upset, not knowing what to do about [...] them "It was Katie [...] arried today, however [...] ecided to go ahead, [...] emony in our chur[...] nice hotel for the [...] funeral home the[...]

We [...] or Katie's funeral i[...] have her flown ba[...] s Katie's wish to be [...] out River and I honoured her wish.

My brother Casabianca, we always called him Cas

Majors Harold and Marion Bungay officiated at her funeral. They are our special friends, and Marion and Katie were like sisters. We were friends from the first day we met at the Salvation Army training college. We were closer than most families and enjoyed our friendship .

Mike and Deanna were also there. Mike, Bill, and Tim were pallbearers for Katie's memorial service. It was helpful having all my children with me during these difficult days.

Chapter 14 – New Assignments and Relationships

After Katie passed away, I became ill and had to get tests done at the hospital.

I was so sick I couldn't travel back to Newfoundland for her burial. It was important for her family and friend to have a memorial service for her in Trout River. As per Katie's wish, I had her flown back to Newfoundland to be buried by her mother in Trout River.

The doctor put me on medication for a nervous condition. I was on Ativan that kept me high most of the time. At that time, I didn't realize that this medication was addictive. I was depending on it daily to get me through. I was lost since a part of me had died when Katie passed away. It was very difficult for me to go on with my life, without her by my side.

I didn't care if I lived or died. I was in so much agony. I was angry at God for taking her from me. I was in darkness and didn't know where to turn. The only consolation I had was the fact that my children were always there for me when and if I needed them.

It was almost impossible for me to continue in Penticton as the corps officer and pastor, without Katie. I was disappointed in The Salvation Army for leaving me there for eight months before transferring me to another appointment. There were times I couldn't function and had to take a month off and focus on myself and my future.

I had many good friends in Penticton, but it was not the same without Katie. There were times, when I came home to the quarters and it was dark and the house was empty, that I dreaded going inside alone.

I was going through a case of depression, and it looked like there was no way out. I was in agony daily and was sure I had a serious illness.

I finally got transferred to Vancouver in June, appointed to a special project.

The Salvation Army was building a hospice in Richmond, and I was appointed as its executive director. I worked with different groups in Vancouver who had donated large sums of money to this project. This appointment was very difficult for me to adjust. Each day I went to my Office at DHQ and waited for instructions and direction from the DHQ staff. It was a slow process, with very little happening with the construction of the Hospice.

Back then, the Army had strict rules regarding officers when it came to marriage. An officer had to marry another officer, with no exceptions. I met a colleague, Major Joanne Bellamy, who was divorced. We had a lot in common related to the Army, so we decided to get married.

I was transferred to Winnipeg, as a chaplain at the Grace Hospital. This was a challenge for me as I was still going through the grieving process. I tried to settle into my new appointment, but I struggled. At times, when I was on call, I would go to the hospital late at night during an emergency. If the patient passed away, it was my responsibility to inform the relatives. Also, at times, I was responsible for getting deceased persons out of the morgue vault for relatives who were coming to see them. I found this very difficult and knew I couldn't continue in this appointment.

Major Jean Moulton came from Toronto to Winnipeg for a program audit. She was head of the Health Services for The Salvation Army across Canada. She knew all this was difficult for me and said that she would not be able to do it. Her husband had passed away a couple of years previously. I didn't ask to be moved even though I found it difficult.

The end of May, Joanne and I received our farewell orders and were appointed to Toronto. Joanne was appointed as the executive director at the women's shelter in Brampton and I was given the role of director at the Maxwell Meighen Centre in downtown Toronto. The Meighen Centre had a capacity for five hundred homeless clients daily. This was a new challenge for me; however, I had a great working relationship with the executive director, Major Roy Snow, and his staff.

During the first year together, Joanne and I realized that we had a lot in common regarding our work, but our relationship didn't come together as it should. We respected each other and were busy caught up in our work. Before the end of the second year, we both realized that our relationship was strained and agreed amicably that we should go our separate ways.

We notified the Divisional Commander and assumed we could continue as officers. The commander, Colonel Max Feener told us that in the United Kingdom, officers who separated could continue to work in separate appointments. We wrote to THQ and advised them of our plans. That went over like a lead balloon.

Major Wayne Pritchett, the head of programs, informed us he would check it out and decide. A couple of months later, he wrote us a letter, stating that in the UK they do let officers continue when they separated, however in Canada it was their decision regarding our future officership.

He said we would have to set the date for our retirement from the Army. We were very disappointed with that decision. We both retired in 2003 and went our separate ways.

Joanne and I remain friends and respect each other for the decision we made. She moved to Winnipeg, and I moved back to Peterborough. It was difficult to live on a Salvation Army pension and if it weren't for my daughters I would not have survived. I would have had to go to a shelter to live.

In 2004, I went to work for the Salvation Army

at their Men's Centre in Windsor as their maintenance supervisor. I really appreciated this position as it increased my funds so I could live decently. Major Clyde Guy, my special friend, hired me for this position.

After a year in this role, I received a call from The Salvation Army in Peterborough, asking me if I would consider a position at the corps as the coordinator of their chaplaincy and correctional program. The only drawback was the salary, which was much less than I received in Windsor.

I decided to take this position. I moved back to Peterborough and started working two days a week at the so-called super jail in Lindsay, one day at the Warkworth Institution, and two days at the office, doing counselling and administration work.

I found it difficult to make ends meet with my income. I received a call from Major Arch Simmonds in Midland. He was looking for a chaplain for the super-jail in Penetanguishene since The Salvation Army had a contract with the institution. He asked if I knew anyone who was qualified and could recommend for this position. The government had specific requirements for this position and the person would have to be approved with the multi-faith organization for Ontario. I asked him about the salary range they were offering, and he wasn't sure. He asked me what I thought was reasonable. I told him in order to get someone qualified, they would have to pay at least $50,000 annually. He thought that was reasonable and asked me if I would accept this position. I told him I would need to put in my notice in Peterborough.

    I asked them if they would raise my salary a little so I could would stay in Peterborough, but they said no. I was only getting $13.00 an hr.

I went to Midland for an interview and was offered the position as the chaplain in the super jail in Penetanguishene. I accepted the position and agreed on a salary of $46,000. I went back to Peterborough and put in my notice. They weren't happy, but I couldn't survive on what they were paying me.

It was funny to some degree. The Salvation Army wouldn't let me and Joanne continue in ministry, but now they were paying me triple what I received as a single officer to minister in an institution.

One day at the super-jail, I received a call from the unit supervisor to come to the unit. A young Muslim inmate was going through a difficult time as he had just lost his grandmother. They put him in a holding area called a bubble and we sat there going over his issues. Without warning, a fight broke out outside his cell. A guard was trying to get an inmate into his cell before lockdown. He refused and took a swing at the guard. The guard had him face down on the floor, when the door opened to the bubble I was in and they started filling it with inmates until this incident was over.

Here I am sitting with this Muslim guy when a huge Black guy looked down at me and said, "You are safe with us, Major."

Then the unit supervisor saw me in with the inmates and shouted out to his staff, "Get him out of there!"

They opened the cell unit and I walked out. I said to him "I'm okay."

He replied, "It doesn't matter. My ass would be on the line if something happened to you in with these inmates."

I thought it was funny. I didn't feel threatened by the inmates as they always looked out for anyone in a Salvation Army uniform.

During my second year the corps officers, Majors Marie and Arch Simmons were always trying to match me up with a woman. One day, Marie said to me, "There is a beautiful woman attending the corps and you should check her out."

They invited me to do a message on Good Friday and seated me out front on the platform so I could see this woman they were referring to.

That was the first time I saw Ann Earle. She was an extremely attractive woman who was widowed and living alone.

I called her about a week later and, invited her out for coffee. Ann was concerned about meeting in public for the first time as people like to gossip, so she invited me to her house for coffee. She felt it was better to meet in private and get to know each other without nosey people questioning her. It was a good visit and we realized that we had a lot in common and decided to see each other on a regular basis. Ann was a gracious lady, who treated everyone with respect.

Everyone who met Ann liked her right away. We dated for over a year and grew close in our relationship. Ann's first husband was also a Newfie and I think she had a soft spot for Newfies.

A year later, we decided to get married in Midland and had a private celebration for our families and close friends. We always enjoyed visiting Newfoundland after we were married. Ann's late husband had family in Victoria Newfoundland and we visited them ever year. They welcomed us and appreciated our visits.

We usually toured the island and stayed in Newfoundland for at least a month each year.

A year after we were married, I received my layoff notice because the government was debating whether they should renew their contract for chaplaincy with the Army. The first of April, I received my layoff notice that would take effect the end of March.

I waited until March 30th before they had a contract signed and on the last day I worked, they called me in saying the contract was renewed.

There were certain clauses in the contract that made it difficult for me to do my work as it should be done. When I first moved to Midland the super jail was operated by a private company. They respected the chaplain and The Salvation Army and provided whatever we needed to do our ministry. They gave us computers, and office equipment that we needed, also access to inmate files and their property as we provided clothing for them upon release and for court appearances.

When the government took over the operation of the institution everything changed. I was denied access to the computer system, had to log everything I did on paper. I didn't have access to the system and was restricted and denied access to the inmates' property. Without staff supervision, it was very difficult for me to do my ministry and provide service to the inmates. I informed the corps officer of the situation and advised him that he needed to address these issues before the Army signed a new contract for the coming year. Apparently, he didn't see it as important so he accepted a new contract with a few more dollars extra, with no access for me to do my work properly. He lacked experience in dealing with the government and gave in to their demands instead of supporting the Salvation Army chaplain. I could not do my ministry as required.

That was the main reason I decided to retire and not continue as the chaplain.

Ann and I had discussed it at length during March and we decided that I should retire, so I did when the contract ended. After I left, they hired Rob Knighton, who had no experience in prison ministry and the Army went along with the government system.

We returned to Peterborough often and Ann really enjoyed the worship at the church. We decided to buy a house in Peterborough and move. That summer in August, we purchased a new house on Abound Crescent. It had been built two years earlier. We moved in and really enjoyed our new location. We visited Newfoundland each year and spent time with her late husband's family and my relatives.

I continued to work for The Salvation Army Correctional Services in Peterborough. I had a contract with them for the home arrest program. I was an electronic specialist and was responsible for installing electronic ankle bracelets on clients who were doing their sentence at home under the home arrest program.

I did this program for eight years, until the federal government legalized marijuana. Then the dynamics changed for this program; clients weren't getting charged for using marijuana, so my case load diminished monthly.

It came to a point where it wasn't financially feasible for me to continue, so I didn't renew my contract with The Salvation Army in Toronto.

Ann and I enjoyed travelling together and rented a house in Florida for a month each winter. We looked forward to getting away from Canada during the winter. It also gave me an opportunity to play golf in Florida. We also enjoyed visiting Clearwater beach and attending The Salvation Army Corps in Clearwater.

We were married for eight years when Ann's health took a turn for the worst. Everything was going great until February 2015, then Ann had some health issues and wasn't feeling well. She continued to get worse, so I called an ambulance, and they took her to the Peterborough Regional Health Centre.

After several tests, they decided she needed her gall bladder removed so they scheduled a laparoscopic surgery for the next day. The doctor told us she would only be in for a day, then would go home. Two days later, she started to get worse, throwing up. They decided to operate to see if they could find out what was happening.

After the laparoscopic surgery, they told us her upper bowel had been cut when they removed her gall bladder, so they patched it when they did complete surgery. After two days, she still wasn't feeling better. They did a scan and decided to send her to a specialist at Toronto General Hospital. We were disappointed in the doctors in Peterborough, to say the least.

The surgeon in Toronto advised me they needed to go in and see what was going on with the surgery she had in Peterborough. What they found was horrifying. Her lower bowels were dead. They did a double colostomy and informed me if Ann didn't rebound in twenty-four hours, she wouldn't make it.

Her bowels never recovered, even after doing a vein transplant to revive it. We were devastated. They wanted to unhook her from the machines, but I refused. Within three to four days, Ann passed away.

As far as I was concerned, they butchered her at the Peterborough hospital, and no one was held accountable for their neglect. I was extremely disappointed in the medical doctors at the hospital. Again, I was alone and had to go on with my life. This was the second time I had lost someone I loved; it was heart-breaking. And I had to go through the grieving process again.

We enjoyed our relationship for eight years and our visits to Newfoundland each year. We also went to Florida for a month each winter. We enjoyed travelling and always drove everywhere and made it a part of our vacation.

Ann has been gone now for six years, in March 2021; I still have mixed feelings towards the medical staff at Peterborough Hospital. The only things that keep me going daily are my family and special friends that I treasure.

Life is never the same when you lose your partner and try to continue on your own. It is difficult when you are trying to start a new life and don't have someone special in your life to share with.

I have several health issues. I am diabetic; I had open heart surgery more than ten years ago and a triple bypass. Now that I am seventy-six years old, my energy is low and can't do a lot of things that I enjoyed. Wood turning was a hobby that I enjoyed doing, but due to the dust I can't do it as often as I'd like. But life is good, and I try to enjoy every day that the good Lord gives me breath. Each one is a new challenge that we face in life; I am grateful for my family and friends. We don't know what the future holds for us daily. I just feel grateful for the years God has blessed me with. I thank him daily for his grace and mercy.

As I look back over the years I realize that I could have made many changes, however I am grateful for all the opportunities I had in ministry. Education is very important, and I had the privilege to study at a number of universities across Canada.

I am grateful for the challenges I had through life and appreciate every blessing that comes my way.

The End